Cambridge Elements

Elements in Religion and Monotheism
edited by
Paul K. Moser
Loyola University Chicago
Chad Meister
Bethel University

ISLAM AND MONOTHEISM

Celene Ibrahim
Groton School

CAMBRIDGE
UNIVERSITY PRESS

CAMBRIDGE
UNIVERSITY PRESS

Shaftesbury Road, Cambridge CB2 8EA, United Kingdom

One Liberty Plaza, 20th Floor, New York, NY 10006, USA

477 Williamstown Road, Port Melbourne, VIC 3207, Australia

314–321, 3rd Floor, Plot 3, Splendor Forum, Jasola District Centre, New Delhi – 110025, India

103 Penang Road, #05–06/07, Visioncrest Commercial, Singapore 238467

Cambridge University Press is part of Cambridge University Press & Assessment, a department of the University of Cambridge.

We share the University's mission to contribute to society through the pursuit of education, learning and research at the highest international levels of excellence.

www.cambridge.org
Information on this title: www.cambridge.org/9781108986519

DOI: 10.1017/9781108986007

First published 2022

A catalogue record for this publication is available from the British Library.

ISBN 978-1-108-98651-9 Paperback
ISSN 2631-3014 (online)
ISSN 2631-3006 (print)

Islam and Monotheism

Elements in Religion and Monotheism

DOI: 10.1017/9781108986007
First published online: September 2022

Celene Ibrahim
Groton School

Author for correspondence: Celene Ibrahim, cibrahim@groton.org

Abstract: Monotheism (*tawḥīd*) – as attested to by the cosmos, known through reason, explicated in revelation, and exemplified by the lives of the righteous – forms the core of the Islamic worldview. A conviction of this unadulterated monotheism unifies Muslims across time and place; it is found in the core profession of faith (the *shahāda*) and reinforced by thousands of Qur'anic verses and prophetic teachings. Drawing on the Qur'anic discourse, sayings of the Prophet Muḥammad, and select theological works, this Element provides a concise and accessible introduction to the most fundamental concept in Islamic thought. The Element explains the nature and attributes of God and examines how *tawḥīd* informs conceptions of truth, morality, piety, and virtue.

Keywords: Islam, Qur'an, God, *tawḥīd*, monotheism

ISBNs: 9781108986519 (PB), 9781108986007 (OC)
ISSNs: 2631-3014 (online), 2631-3006 (print)

Contents

1 Introduction

The Qur'an contains hundreds of statements on the nature of God and the nature of the human being in relation to God. Sayings and teachings attributed to the Prophet Muḥammad also elaborate concepts related to monotheism. These prophetic sayings have reached subsequent generations through a combination of oral and written transmissions in the form of hadith reports. Religious scholarship also includes creedal works that systematize Qur'anic and prophetic teachings on the nature of God.[1] Muslim theologians, scholars, teachers, and preachers then relate the core principles of the Islamic monotheistic worldview to the pressing social issues of their age.

This Element draws upon the Qur'an and other foundational Islamic sources, upon select premodern treatises, and upon a variety of contemporary theological and scholarly works in English and Arabic to explicate basic Muslim understandings of monotheism, or *tawḥīd*. I explain Qur'anic arguments on the nature of God, outline human beings' capacity to understand this nature, and describe the myriad ways that human beings either fail to comprehend aspects of *tawḥīd* or fail to act appropriately upon their knowledge. I consider how deluded beliefs about God lead to faulty moral action and detail how appropriate understanding of the nature of God inspires insight and upright behavior. I emphasize this connection between practices of character formation and processes of inculcating monotheistic conviction, showing how a proper conception of God's nature encourages meritorious conduct, and vice versa, in a self-perpetuating cycle. Thus, in explicating the Qur'anic worldview, this Element highlights the profound link between God-consciousness and pious practice.

The word *tawḥīd* does not appear in the Qur'an itself; it is a verbal noun (*maṣdar*), the literal sense of which is "to deem or to declare one." It is used more generally in reference to God's oneness itself. The number one in Arabic is also derived from the same root, namely *w-ḥ-d*. The concept of *tawḥīd* simultaneously describes God and points toward a person's active awareness of God. The first part of the *shahāda*, the testimony of faith and the first pillar (*rukn*) of Islam – the assertion that "there is no god [i.e., nothing worthy of worship] other than God" – is an external declaration of *tawḥīd*. This act of "witnessing"

[1] Famous early works in this genre include that of the Sunni scholar Aḥmad b. Muḥammad al-Ṭaḥāwī (d. AH 321 / 933 CE) and Abū l-Ḥasan ʿAlī b. al-Ḥusayn b. Mūsā b. Bābawayh al-Qummī (d. AH 329 / 941 CE), popularly known as al-Shaykh al-Ṣadūq. See Hamza Yusuf, *The Creed of Imam al-Ṭaḥāwī (al-ʿAqīdah al-Ṭaḥāwiyya)* (Berkeley, CA: Zaytuna Institute, 2007); see also *The Book of Divine Unity* (*Kitāb al-tawḥīd*), trans. Ali Adam, ed. Michal Mumisa and Mahmood Dhalla (Birmingham, UK: Al-Mahdi Institute, 2013). A helpful reference work containing selections from classical exegesis is Feras Hamza, Sajjad Rizvi, and Farhana Mayer, eds., *An Anthology of Qur'anic Commentaries, Volume I: On the Nature of the Divine*. Institute of Ismaili Studies Qur'anic Studies Series 5 (New York: Oxford University Press, 2008).

conveyed by the *shahāda* signifies a profound experiential knowing – a state of being that is the apex of human spiritual acumen and the goal of pious practice.

Certain core beliefs regarding this concept of *tawḥīd*, unadulterated monotheism, organize Islamic thought and unify Muslims across different backgrounds and sects. These general, widely held aspects of monotheism in Islamic thought are my focus in this Element. In the notes, I direct readers to further academic resources on the finer points of theological debate.

2 Conceptualizing *Tawḥīd*: God in Islamic Theology

Muslims developed overlapping fields of theological discourse known as *ʿaqīda* and *kalām*. *ʿAqīda* is a common Arabic word that signifies belief or creed; its root meaning is "to knit, to knot, to tie, to join," though it can also mean to resolve something or to make up one's mind, among other derived meanings. In slight contrast, *kalām* (derived from the root *k-l-m*, lit. "speech") is a branch of speculative theology that emerged in response to Muslim encounters with Greek philosophy and other worldviews. Knowledge of the basic aspects of belief (*ʿaqīda*) is understood to be incumbent on each intellectually mature Muslim. In *kalām* discourses, theologians debate their subtle creedal differences in erudite philosophical terms. Ordinary Muslims without specialized training could even be discouraged from reading *kalām* works, lest the finer points of dispute on the precise nature and attributes of God lead to unnecessary confusion.[2]

Muslim theological treatises frequently discuss the following major themes: (1) the nature and attributes of God (*ilāhiyyāt*), (2) the nature and functions of prophethood (*nubuwwāt*), and (3) the nonmaterial world (*ghaybiyyāt*), including eschatological themes. Here, I first offer a concise explanation of the divine attributes. I organize the discussions of God's nature into three broad topics: (1) God as the supreme being, (2) God as the singular entity for worship, and (3) God's names and attributes. The ultimate reality of God is, of course, beyond such a conceptual division; these thematic categories are merely vantage points for describing the Real One, the True One. Subsequent sections of this Element discuss the functions of prophethood (Section 3.1) and eschatology (Section 4.3) in relation to Islamic monotheism (*tawḥīd*).

[2] For longer works detailing the historical development and the finer theological divergences found in the *kalām* discourse, see Sabine Schmidtke, ed., *The Oxford Handbook of Islamic Theology* (Oxford: Oxford University Press, 2016); Tim Winter, ed., *The Cambridge Companion to Classical Islamic Theology* (Cambridge: Cambridge University Press, 2008); and Ramon Harvey, *Transcendent God, Rational World: A Māturīdī Theology* (Edinburgh: Edinburgh University Press, 2021). For an introductory history of the origins of Islamic thought through the contemporary period, see Fitzroy Morrissey, *A Short History of Islamic Thought* (New York: Oxford University Press, 2022).

2.1 Ultimate Sustainer and Supreme Being

In Islamic thought, God is the Creator, the Controller, the Commander, the Supreme One, and more. Everything in existence originates according to God's will, finds continual existence according to God's will, and ceases to exist according to God's will. God is the only True Existence, the Living, the One through whom all other beings and things have contingent existence and life. This aspect of God that pertains to His lordship over all of creation is sometimes referred to in theological treatises as *tawḥīd al-rubūbiyya* (unity of lordship). Many Qur'anic verses emphasize God's ultimate lordship, as we can see, for instance, in Sūrat al-Ḥadīd (Q 57), which offers this summary:

> Whatever is in the heavens and the earth glorifies God, and He is the Mighty, the Wise.
>
> To Him belongs sovereignty over the heavens and the earth. He gives life and causes death, and He is powerful over all things.
>
> He is the First, the Last, the Outward, and the Inward; and He is Knower of all things. (Q al-Ḥadīd 57:1–3)

God transcends time, phenomena, the physicality of human sensory perception, and any spatial measure or physical confine. Accordingly, the Subtle One exists beyond a body, beyond gender. Though human beings might employ gendered language, God is beyond male or female, as these are qualities of beings in the created sphere. "Allah is beyond He and She, Him and Her, and even It," observes the contemporary Islamic historian Bruce Lawrence.[3] God is not embodied the way other beings are embodied; therefore, when the Qur'an refers to particular body parts of God (eyes, face, hand, fist, etc.), Muslim theologians take these references either metaphorically or at face value but without drawing an ontological likeness to embodiment in human terms, "without asking how."[4]

The creative power of God – known as the Maker, the Fashioner, the Originator, and more – brings creation from nonexistence. The Qur'an asks rhetorically: "Were they created from naught? Or are they the creators? Or did they create the heavens and the earth? Nay, but they have no certainty. Do they possess the treasuries of your Lord? Or are they in control?" (Q al-Ṭūr 35–37). In contrast, human forms of creation and production are mere transformations or manipulations of previously existing substances. In her recent book exploring *tawḥīd* in daily devotion, Yamina Bouguenaya, an astrophysicist, scholar of Islamic theology, and specialist in the works of the Kurdish theologian Said

[3] Bruce Lawrence, *Who Is Allah?* (Chapel Hill: University of North Carolina Press, 2015), 3.

[4] This theological position is known as *tafwīḍ* (lit. "consigning [to God]").

Nursi (1876–1960), responds to a scientific materialist perspective of worldly phenomena: "Indeed, there is order and everything comes into existence through something else. However, this does not mean that the causes themselves *create*. The Quran repeatedly calls us to think and see that causes themselves are being created – they cannot sustain their own existence let alone produce anything else."[5]

All created things, without exception, come into existence in accord with the divine will and return to nonexistence: "Truly it is He who originates and brings back" (Q al-Burūj 85:13). Even the very bonds of the universe depend on God sustaining them: "Truly God holds fast the heavens and the earth, lest they break apart. And were they to break apart, none would maintain them after Him; truly He is Clement, Forgiving" (Q Fāṭir 35:41). Ownership and dominion (*mulk*), moreover, belong solely to the Supreme One. Human ownership and rule are restricted, temporary, and bound by the inherent limits of the human being's fundamental condition as a perpetually vulnerable, mortal creature. God, in contrast, has supreme ownership and absolute will as the "Possessor of the Throne, the Glorious, Doer of whatever He will" (Q al-Burūj 85:15–16).

God is utterly unique. That nothing bears a likeness to the Real One is central to the Qur'anic discourse. For instance, the Qur'an contrasts the independent nature of God's existence with the fundamental dependence of creatures: "O humankind! You are needful of God; and He is the Self-Sufficient, the Praised" (Q Fāṭir 35:15). Even the sexual bifurcation of species and cycles of reproduction stand in stark contrast to God, who has no partner, no equal, no progenitor: "The Originator of the heavens and the earth, He [God] has appointed for you mates from among yourselves and has appointed mates also among cattle. He multiplies you thereby; naught is like unto Him, yet He is the Hearer, the Seer" (Q al-Shūrā 42:11).[6]

The nature of God's uncompromised independence and self-sufficiency, in contrast to the absolute dependency of human beings and other created entities, is foundational to the Islamic worldview. One of the shortest surahs of the Qur'an, known commonly as Sūrat al-Ikhlāṣ (Q 112), in its entirety, is a concise explication of this facet of God's nature:

> Say, "He, God, is One,
> God, the Eternally Sufficient to Himself,
> He begets not, nor was He begotten.
> And none is like unto Him." (Q al-Ikhlāṣ 112:1–4)

[5] Yamina Bouguenaya, *Living with Genuine Tawhid: Witnessing the Signs of God through Qur'anic Guidance* (Charlottesville, VA: Receiving Nur, 2016), 27.

[6] For further discussion of divine unicity and human sexed bodies, see Celene Ibrahim, *Women and Gender in the Qur'an* (New York: Oxford University Press, 2020), 20–25.

The British philosopher of religion Roger Trigg summarizes this concept in philosophical metaphysics: "A feature of God's otherness is His difference from Creation. Theism is not pantheism. God's immanence cannot be stressed to the detriment of the idea of transcendence. This implies the total distinctness of God from any forms of human understanding. He is metaphysically 'self-subsistent.'"[7]

In contrast to the utter self-subsistence of God, human existence is defined by finitude, frailty, and dependency. Human beings are fundamentally dependent on their Creator, the Controller and Lord of the universe, by design. God's lordship is absolute over humans and all of creation: "To Him belongs all that dwells in the night and in the day, and He is the Hearing, the Knowing" (Q al-Anʿām 6:13). God is supremely Knowing, not just of the universals but of particulars too: "God knows what every female bears, how wombs diminish and how they increase; everything with Him is according to a measure – Knower of the unseen and the seen, the Great, the Exalted" (Q al-Raʿd 13:8–9). Nothing exists but that God possesses complete knowledge of its nature and attributes: "With Him [God] are the keys of the unseen. None knows them but He. He knows what is on land and sea; no leaf falls but that He knows it, nor any seed in the dark recesses of the earth, nor anything moist or dry, but that it is in a clear register" (Q al-Anʿām 6:59).

As Creator and Sustainer, God encompasses knowledge of the states and desires of every human being and each creature, in full and effortlessly: "He it is who originates creation then brings it back, and that is most easy for Him; unto Him belongs the loftiest description in the heavens and on the earth, and He is the Mighty, the Wise" (Q al-Rūm 30:27). Moreover, in the Qur'anic depiction, God is aware of the state of a given human being even more than the human being knows herself/himself. The following verse explains this idea using the imagery of the blood vessels that connect the heart and brain: "We [God] indeed created the human being, and We know what his soul whispers to him; and We are nearer to him than his jugular vein" (Q Qāf 50:16).

2.2 Singular Entity for Worship

This next facet of Islamic monotheism concerns God as the Sustainer, the sole entity worthy of worship (*ʿibāda*). Worship includes not only acts of veneration but also dispositions and desires relating to love, hope, obedience, and awe. In the Islamic worldview, worship consists of embodied practices and

[7] Roger Trigg, *Monotheism and Religious Diversity* (Cambridge: Cambridge University Press, 2020), 30.

intentions. God is the True, the Real, and the human being engages in acts of worship with a sincere longing to draw nearer to True Reality (*al-Ḥaqq*). This veneration of God is the very raison d'être of human existence. Directing worship toward intermediary beings other than or alongside God is the epitome of theological corruption. The Arabic word *ḥaqq* (pl. *ḥuqūq*), in addition to signifying a name of God, also pertains to the rights that entities have with respect to other entities. In a widely circulated hadith, the Prophet Muḥammad explains the rights that God has over people and the rights that God has given people over Himself: "God's right on His servants is that they worship Him alone and not associate with Him anything; the right of the servant on God is that He should not punish anyone who does not associate with Him anything."[8] It might seem odd to think of human beings having rights over God, but, in the Islamic understanding, these rights are derivative of a covenant through which God has willingly bound Himself (see, for instance, Q al-Anʿām 6:12). God's power is tempered with His promise of mercy for those who earn His favor.

The command to worship God appears throughout the Qur'an. The Arabic root *ʿ-b-d*, from which the concept of worship is derived, has a range of meanings, including to be a servant or to be enslaved to something or someone. All entities are in a state of subservience to God, in accord with their fundamental design: "To Him belongs whoever is in the heavens and on the earth; all are devoutly obedient to Him" (Q al-Rūm 30:26). Another set of verses evokes the example of thunder: "The thunder hymns His [God's] praise, as do the angels, in awe of Him. He sends forth the thunderbolts and strikes therewith whomsoever He will. Yet they dispute concerning God, and He is severe in wrath" (Q al-Raʿd 13:13). The command to revere God is addressed to all humankind in the Qur'an:

> O humankind! Worship your Lord, who created you, and those who were before you, that perhaps you may be reverent.
>
> [Worship] He who made for you the earth a place of repose and the sky a canopy and [who] sent water from the sky by which He brought forth fruits for your provision. So do not set up equals to God knowingly.
>
> (Q al-Baqara 2:21–22)

This notion of setting up equals to God refers to an individual who worships something or someone beyond God, the worship of which brings no benefit:

[8] Variations of this hadith occur in well-known collections; for instance, see the entries on the Sunnah.com website for *al-Bukhārī* (https://sunnah.com/bukhari:2856) and *Muslim* (https://sunnah.com/muslim:30b).

> To Him [God] is the supplication of truth. Those whom they supplicate apart from Him answer them not in the least, save as one who stretches forth his palms toward water that it may reach his mouth, though it never reaches him. And the supplication of the deniers is not but in error. (Q al-Raʿd 13:14)

Human beings do not have a choice about their fundamental state of subservience to the will of God: "And to God prostrates whoever is in the heavens and on the earth, willingly or unwillingly, as do their shadows in the morning and the evening" (Q al-Raʿd 13:15). People might be compelled to revere God, but they do have a choice about their disposition toward this intrinsic command. Some human beings earn God's favor through their proactive subservience: "And among humankind is one who sells his soul seeking God's good pleasure, and God is Kind to the servants [*al-ʿibād*]" (Q al-Baqara 2:207). God is knowledgeable of – and is even described as appreciating – reverence:

> Reverence God as much as you are able. Listen, obey, and spend; that is better for your souls. And whoever is shielded from the avarice of his soul, it is he who shall prosper.
>
> If you lend to God a goodly loan, He will multiply it for you and forgive you; and God is Appreciative, Clement,
>
> Knower of the Unseen and the seen, the Mighty, the Wise.
>
> (Q al-Taghābun 64:16–18)

When a creature worships with sincere devotion, God is Responsive (*al-Mujīb*). In a famous Qur'anic verse, God instructs the Prophet Muḥammad with respect to the faithful: "When My servants ask you [Prophet] about Me [God], truly I am near. I [God] respond to the invocation of the supplicant when he invokes Me. So let them respond to Me and have faith in Me, that they may be led aright" (Q al-Baqara 2:186). When a human being responds to the perennial invitation to worship, God responds affirmatively.

In an essay on worship in Islamic thought, William Chittick, a contemporary scholar of Islamic theology and mysticism, summarizes the centrality of this pure monotheism to all subsequent thought: "Islamic theology – God-talk in all its forms – is concerned with clarifying the reality of the Object of Worship, the Absolute *Ḥaqq*, so that people can relate to it in the right and appropriate manner."[9] The essence of piety is beseeching God with a pure realization of utter dependence: "And call not on another god along with God. There is no god other than Him! All things perish, save His Face. Judgment belongs to Him, and to Him will you be returned" (Q al-Qaṣaṣ 28:88). God is the Self-Sufficient and does not require veneration to be the Supreme or the Holy. God's attributes are

9 William C. Chittick, "Worship," in *The Cambridge Companion to Classical Islamic Theology*, ed. Tim Winter, 218–236 (Cambridge: Cambridge University Press, 2008), 221.

intrinsic and are not affected by the actions of created entities. Human beings, by contrast, are impacted in myriad ways by the quality of their servanthood, and they differ from one another in the magnitude of their veneration. Among all the ways that people differ from one another – differences such as ethnicity, gender, and so forth – the most critical difference is the quality of their reverence: "O humankind! We [God] made you peoples and tribes that you may come to know one another. Surely the most noble of you before God are the most reverent of you. Truly God is Knowing, Aware" (Q al-Ḥujurāt 49:13).

From an Islamic point of view, human beings are not the only entities endowed with a capacity for veneration. Entities can express worship beyond what is readily discerned by an ordinary person: "The seven heavens, and the earth, and whoever is in them glorify Him [God]. And there is no thing, save that it hymns His praise, though you [human beings] do not understand their praise. Truly He is Clement, Forgiving" (Q al-Isrāʾ 17:44). Most created entities simply venerate God without a conscious choice, with two prominent exceptions mentioned regularly in foundational Islamic sources: humans and *jinn*. *Jinn* are beings of the unseen world to whom God has given the ability to enact their will, as He has similarly given human beings. In an oft-quoted verse of the Qur'an, the voice of God directly indicates the existential purpose of *jinn* and human beings: "I [God] did not create jinn and humankind, except to venerate Me" (Q al-Dhāriyāt 51:56).

God is the Provider for all creatures, the source of sustenance and succor, even if the proximate cause seems to be something material and direct (money, food, a specific person, etc.). The God-conscious person uses these worldly means while relying entirely on the Sustainer. The Qur'an explains that when a person spends of their means for a just cause, for instance, God is particularly generous: "Say, 'Truly my Lord extends provisions for whomever He will among His servants; whatever you have spent, He will replace, and He is the best of providers'" (Q Sabaʾ 34:39). Material means are merely that: they have an ultimate Originator. This source, which is none other than God, is kind, generous, and subtle, but God is also the Withholder and the Constrictor. God is the One who measures out according to divine knowledge and awareness that is well beyond ordinary human comprehension. In Arabic, fate, power, and measurement share a common root (*q-d-r*): God is the One who determines fates, the All-Powerful. "Truly We [God] have created everything according to a measure" (Q al-Qamar 54:49).

In short, the universe that human beings inhabit by the will and power of God is imbued with purpose and cognizance. The extent to which people become aware, discern their God-given purpose, and then fulfill it determines their potential to succeed in life, in Qur'anic terms. True success lies in piety, and piety lies in understanding and proactive surrender to the servitude of the human condition. God's nature is ultimately far beyond human comprehension; however, people can grasp some facets through cognitive and experiential awareness, through engagement with scripture, and through engaging in a process of character refinement as detailed in subsequent sections of this Element. I now turn to a brief synopsis of various names and attributes of God in Islamic thought.

2.3 Possessor of Names and Attributes

Islamic theological treatises typically involve discussions of God's names and qualities (*asmāʾ wa-ṣifāt*). Some scholars consider Allāh a proper name that does not have a morphological derivation. Others consider it a contraction of the definite article *al-* and the word *ilāh*, meaning *god*. The two parts then contract to form the word *Allāh*, signifying "the God" – the One, the only true God. Umar Faruq Abd-Allah, a contemporary Muslim theologian, explains the linguistic origins of the term *Allāh* and the similarities with other Semitic languages:

> Etymologically, *Allāh* comes from the same root as the Biblical words *Elōhîm*, *hā-Elōhîm*, and *hā-Elôh* (all meaning "God") invoked by the Hebrew prophets and the Aramaic and Syriac *Alāhā* ("God") used by John the Baptist and Jesus. *Elōhîm* derives from *elôh* (Hebrew for "god"), and *Alāhā* is an emphatic form of *alāh* (Aramaic/Syriac for "god"), while *Allāh* is connected to *ilāh* (Arabic for "god"). All three of these Semitic words for "god" – *elôh*, *alāh*, and *ilāh* – are etymologically equivalent. The slight modifications between them reflect different pronunciations conforming to the historical pattern of morphological shifts in each tongue. They are akin to the variations we find, for example, between the Latin, Spanish, and Italian words for God (*Deus*, *Dios*, and *Dio*) or the English and German (*God* and *Gott*). *Elōhîm*, *Alāhā*, and *Allāh* are all cognates – sister words – deriving from a common proto-Semitic root, which, according to one standard view, was the root *ʾLH*, conveying the primary sense of "to worship." The fundamental linguistic meaning of the three Abrahamic cognates for God – *Elōhîm*, *Alāhā*, and *Allāh* – is "the one who is worshiped."[10]

By far the most common name for God in the Qur'an is *Allāh*, which is mentioned upward of two thousand times.[11] Many Qur'anic verses mention God by specific names or a series of names:

---

[10] Umar Faruq Abd-Allah, "One God, Many Names" (Chicago, IL: Nawawi Foundation, 2004), 3.

[11] One reliable concordance (https://corpus.quran.com) counts 2,699 instances of the name *Allāh* and 5 instances of the direct address *Allāhumma* (in 3:26, 5:11, 8:23, 10:10, and 39:46). The word *god* (*ilāh*) appears another 147 times, in some instances referring to God and in other instances referring to gods that human beings have fashioned.

> He is God, other than whom there is no god, the Sovereign, the Holy, Peace, the Faithful, the Protector, the Mighty, the Compeller, the Proud. Glory be to Him above the partners they ascribe.
>
> He is God, the Creator, the Maker, the Fashioner; to Him belong the Most Beautiful Names. Whatever is in the heavens and the earth glorifies Him, and He is the Mighty, the Wise. (Q al-Ḥashr 59:23–24)

The concept of God's "most beautiful names" appears in the Qur'an in conjunction with an affirmation of monotheism: "God, there is no god other than Him. To Him belong the Most Beautiful Names" (Q Ṭā Hā 20:8). God's most beautiful names (*asmāʾ Allāh al-ḥusnā*) are often thought to be ninety-nine in number; however, the epithets for God in the Qur'an and hadith extend well beyond that number.[12] In the musnad of Aḥmad b. Ḥanbal (d. AH 241 / 855 CE), an early collection of hadith on which many subsequent scholarly works were based, the Prophet Muḥammad is reported to have prayed to God, saying: "I ask You by every name with which You have named Yourself, revealed in Your book, taught any of Your creation, or reserved for Yourself in the knowledge of the unseen that is with You."[13]

According to other hadith, the Prophet Muḥammad was in the habit of ending his daily prayers by evoking God as the Peace (*al-Salām*): "You are Peace and from you is peace. Blessed are You, Possessor of Glory and Honor."[14] The Arabic root *s-l-m* is the root of the words *Islam* and *Muslim*. The Arabic word *islām* signifies willing surrender to God and the state of peace that results in the heart from this surrender. The word also bears a semantic relationship to the notion of safety, completeness, and freedom from impairment. Surrendering to God, the source of all peace, leads individuals to wholeness, contentment, and fulfillment.

In this way, God has various names that indicate aspects of His essence. Theological works abound with discussions of which names and attributes are the most essential. Theologians often consider these essential attributes characteristics of God's essence (*dhāt*), as contrasted with attributes of action.

[12] For the number ninety-nine, see the entry on the Sunnah.com website for *al-Bukhārī* (https://sunnah.com/bukhari:2736), on the authority of the companion of the Prophet Muḥammad, Abū Hurayra (ʿAbd al-Raḥmān b. Ṣakhr, d. ca. AH 59 / 678 CE). A list of ninety-nine specific names is narrated on the authority of the Prophet Muḥammad's cousin, son-in-law, esteemed caliph, and first Shia imam, ʿAlī b. Abī Ṭālib (d. AH 40 / 661 CE). For an academic analysis of premodern works on the most beautiful names, see Daniel Gimaret, *Les noms divins en Islam: Exégèse lexicographique et théologique* (Paris: Cerf, 1988).

[13] See the entry on the Sunnah.com website for the musnad of Aḥmad b. Ḥanbal (https://sunnah.com/hisn:120). See also Abd-Allah, "One God, Many Names," 4.

[14] This hadith was transmitted on the authority of the Prophet Muḥammad's wife ʿĀʾisha bt. Abī Bakr (d. AH 58 / 678 CE); see the entry on the Sunnah.com website for *Muslim* (https://sunnah.com/muslim:592a).

Countless variations on the essential aspects of the divine essence are found in Muslim theological works and treatises that expound on the meanings and significances of the various divine names. In the Qur'an itself, God as "the Merciful, the Compassionate" (*al-raḥmān al-raḥīm*) appears at the beginning of all but one of the surahs, in the opening surah of the Qur'an (*al-Fātiḥa*), and in many other verses. For example, this verse connects absolute monotheism to the compassionate nature of God: "Your God is one God, there is no god other than Him, the Compassionate, the Merciful" (Q al-Baqara 2:263). God is, by essential nature, merciful toward creation: "He has prescribed Mercy for Himself" (Q al-Anʿām 6:12, partial citation). The word signifying God's mercy (*raḥma*) is mentioned 114 times in the Qur'an. God as *Raḥmān* is mentioned an additional 57 times, and God as *Raḥīm* is mentioned 115 times; this count does not include the instances of *al-Raḥmān* and *al-Raḥīm* in the *basmala*, the declaration of God's compassionate nature that opens 113 surahs.[15]

Human beings struggle to fathom the divine nature and must understand through similitudes. Muslim scholars are quick to point out that the divine attributes are not like the human experience of these qualities. However, a shade of resemblance enables human beings to begin to comprehend the meaning of God's names. God possesses the attributes in their most total, truest manifestation, and entities in the world reflect specific attributes of God as the moon reflects the light of the sun. For instance, though people can acquire some knowledge of discrete subjects, God is the Knower of all the particulars. Human beings, for another example, may demonstrate compassion toward one another or other sentient beings; however, even the collective human expression of compassion does not approximate the extent of God's compassion. Similarly, though God is beyond gender and possesses no offspring, one hadith explicates the quality of divine compassion by pointing to the caring actions of a nursing mother.[16] God's utter transcendence and power are balanced with an intimate, forbearing, and loving nature that pervades the cosmos: "He [God] is the Forgiving, the Loving" (Q al-Burūj 85:14).

3 Discerning *Tawḥīd*: Human Awareness of God

The horizon of the human's ability to comprehend God's nature, according to Islamic thought broadly and the Qur'anic discourse specifically, is the theme of this section. I outline how human beings acquire knowledge of God's essence and attributes by drawing on the Qur'an, the hadith, and the Islamic intellectual

[15] *Sūrat al-Tawba* (Q 9) is the only one of the Qur'an's 114 surahs that does not open with the *basmala*, the phrase that evokes God as the Compassionate, the Merciful.

[16] See the entry on the Sunnah.com website for *al-Bukhārī* (https://sunnah.com/bukhari:5999).

tradition broadly. I explain the confluence of reason and revelation as sources of knowledge and explore how self-knowledge can lead to a deeper understanding of God's nature and cosmic truth, according to a basic Muslim understanding. I detail how a person's rational intellect and heart, the seat of esoteric knowledge, work in tandem to yield an awareness of God.

3.1 Prophethood, Revelation, and Guidance

According to Qur'anic and prophetic teaching, each human being's innate disposition (*fiṭra*) guides him/her toward the upright, sound way (*dīn*), the straight path of *tawḥīd*: "Set your face, inclining to the way as a pure monotheist (*ḥanīf*) with the innate disposition (*fiṭra*) on which He originated humankind – there is no altering the creation of God; that is the established way, but most of humankind know not" (Q al-Rūm 30:30). In an Islamic worldview, pure monotheism is not only the essential and original nature of the human being but also the primal state of all sentient and non-sentient existence. According to the Qur'an, the human being's monotheistic disposition is a result of the individual's soul, which, before her earthly existence, bore witness to a primordial pact (*ʿahd*), or covenant (*mīthāq*), wherein God asked: "Am I not your Lord?" (Q al-Aʿrāf 7:172, partial citation), and the pretemporal beings bore witness concerning themselves.[17]

The theological content of revelation, therefore, augments what human beings can discern through their own efforts to reason.[18] Prophets, then, are enlightened individuals who teach the theology of pure monotheism that confirms what is already latent in human consciousness. The Qur'an often speaks of itself and previous revelations as a "reminder"; it merely confirms what is already knowable through inherent spiritual acumen. Enlightened individuals come to humankind as a mercy from God with reminders about the nature of this relationship between creation and God. The Qur'an summarizes this process: "God chooses messengers from among the angels and from among humankind. Truly God is Hearing, Seeing" (Q al-Ḥajj 22:75). The prophets who brought scripture have special status as "messengers" (*rusul*, sing. *rasūl*): "For every community there is a messenger, and when their messenger comes, judgment will be rendered between them with justice, and they will not be wronged"

[17] Some exegetes interpret this verse figuratively and others take it to describe an event before the creation of earthly time. For a brief discussion of the verse's significance, see Nasr et al., *The Study Quran: A New Translation and Commentary* (San Francisco: HarperOne, 2015), 466–469; for a fuller discussion, see Joseph Lumbard, "Covenant and Covenants in the Quran," *Journal of Qur'anic Studies* 17, no. 2 (2015): 1–23.

[18] For probing analysis and extensive further resources, see Carl Sharif El-Tobgui, *Ibn Taymiyya on Reason and Revelation: A Study of Dar' taʿāruḍ al-ʿaql wa-l-naql* (Leiden: Brill, 2020).

(Q Yūnus 10:47). Many Qur'anic narratives relate the experiences of prophets who debate with their people about the nature of God and the parameters of human virtue. Sūrat Ibrāhīm (Q 14), a surah named after the prophet Abraham, relates one such exchange:

> Has not the account come to you of those who came before you – the people of Noah, and ʿĀd, and Thamūd, and those who came after them? None knows them but God. Their messengers brought them clear proofs, but they [the people to whom the prophets were sent] thrust their hands into their mouths and said, "Verily we disbelieve in that wherewith you have been sent, and we are in grave doubt about that to which you call us."
>
> Their messengers said, "Is there any doubt concerning God, the Originator of the heavens and the earth? He calls you that He might forgive some of your shortcomings and grant you reprieve till a term appointed." They said, "You are but human beings like us. You desire to turn us away from that which our fathers used to worship. So, bring us a manifest authority!"
>
> Their messengers said to them, "We are but human beings like yourselves, but God is gracious to whoever He will among His servants. It is not for us to bring you an authority, save by God's leave; so, in God let the faithful trust.
>
> And why should we not trust in God, when He has guided us in our ways? We will surely endure patiently however you may torment us. Let those who trust, trust in God." (Q Ibrāhīm 9–12)

Prophets (*anbiyāʾ* or *nabiyyūn*, sing. *nabī*) do not bring a new scripture but have been sent to remind their people of the previous scriptures, of the signs in nature, and of the intrinsic monotheistic disposition of the human being. In one verse, the Qur'an explains the nature of prophethood to the Prophet Muḥammad himself:

> Truly, We [God] have sent messengers before you. Among them are those whom We have recounted to you, and among them are those whom We have not recounted to you. And it was not for a messenger to bring a sign, save by God's leave. So, when God's command comes, judgment is passed in truth and those who make false claims will then be losers. (Q Ghāfir 40:78)

Scripture appears in specific times and places; however, its message of unadulterated monotheism (of *tawḥīd*) is universal in Muslim understanding. Thus, the messengers may bring a specific new set of rules and regulations for ritual and social interaction, but the basic message of monotheism is consistent across divinely inspired scriptures and the teaching of divinely guided prophets.

Muslim doctrinal theology (*kalām*) examines the nature of divine speech and the relationship between God's speaking and scripture. Is speech a fundamental attribute or an act? How does the temporal dimension of scripture relate to God's existence beyond time? The Qur'an itself does not detail precisely how a spirit (*rūḥ*) mediates between the divine and the material world beyond a few details on the nature of God's messages to human beings generally and to the Prophet Muḥammad specifically:

> It is not for any human being that God should speak to him save by revelation, or from behind a veil, or that He [God] should send a messenger to reveal what He will by His leave. Truly He is Exalted, Wise.
>
> Thus have We [Good] revealed to you [Prophet Muḥammad] a spirit from our command. You knew not what scripture was, nor faith [before this], but We made it a light whereby We guide whomever We will among Our servants. Truly you guide to a straight path,
>
> The path of God, to Whom belongs whatever is in the heavens and whatever is on the earth. Behold! All affairs are destined to God.
>
> (Q al-Shūrā 42:51–53)

As suggested in these verses, prophethood is a special commission yet the prophet is also a human with a host of ordinary human limitations. For instance, the Qur'an relates the words of the Prophet Noah (Nūḥ) to his people: "I say not to you that with me are the treasuries of God; nor do I know the unseen. And I say not that I am an angel; nor do I say of those who are despicable in your eyes 'God will not give them any good' – God knows best what is in their souls – for then [if I said these things] I would indeed be among the wrongdoers" (Q Hūd 11:31).

Similarly, the Qur'an instructs the Prophet Muḥammad that he should explain his own human limitations to his critics as follows: "Say, 'I have no power over what benefit or harm may come to me, save as God wills. Had I knowledge of the unseen, I would have acquired much good and no evil would have touched me. I am naught save a warner and a bearer of glad tidings to a people who have faith'" (Q al-Aʿrāf 7:188).

Prophets, in general, are people of integrity – with a reputation for credibility and honesty – who warn against the consequences of wrongdoing and urge people to lead lives of virtue by following the way of pure monotheism and upright morality. For instance, the Qur'an instructs the Prophet Muḥammad to give the following guidance:

> Say: "Come, I will recite that which your Lord has forbidden you: that you ascribe nothing as a partner to Him, and that you be virtuous toward parents, and that you slay not your children for fear of poverty – We [God] will provide for you and for them – and that you not approach indecencies, whether outward or inward, nor slay the soul that God has made inviolable, save by right. This He has enjoined on you, that haply you may understand.
>
> And approach not the orphan's property, save in the best manner, until he [the male or female orphan] reaches maturity. And observe fully the measure and the balance with justice. We [God] task no soul beyond her capacity. And when you speak, be just, even if it be [against] a kinsperson,

> and fulfill the pact of God. This He has enjoined on you, that haply you may remember.
>
> This indeed is My [God's] path made straight; so follow it, and do not follow other ways, lest they separate you from His [God's] way. This He [God] has enjoined on you that haply you may be reverent."
>
> (Q al-Anʿām 6:151–53)

Prophets are not accountable for the actions of their people. For example, the Qur'an instructs the Prophet Muḥammad on one of many similar instances: "Say, 'O humankind! The truth has come to you from your Lord. Whoever is rightly guided is only rightly guided for the sake of their own soul, and whoever is astray is only astray to its detriment. And I [the prophet] am not a guardian over you'" (Q Yūnus 10:108).

The message of scripture is not just an informational reminder but a source of motivation and comfort. The Qur'an, for instance, describes itself as having somatic and metaphysical effects: "O humankind! There has come to you an exhortation from your Lord, and a cure for that which lies within breasts, and a guidance and a mercy for those who are faithful" (Q Yūnus 10:57). The notion of cultivating piety and purifying the heart to increase its understanding is the subject of many Qur'anic verses and is examined next.

3.2 Conviction and the Straight Path

Tawḥīd is not simply a matter of intellectual discernment and theological speculation. Actions originate in desire, and the seat of desire is the metaphysical heart. According to the Qur'anic worldview, much spiritual perception happens through the sensory knowledge of this spiritual heart, the seat of intuition and the locus of metaphysical perception. The contemporary American-Muslim scholar Hamza Yusuf draws a connection between the vital function of the physical heart and the essential function of the metaphorical one:

> It [the heart] yearns always to remember God, the Exalted. But when God is not remembered, when human beings forget God, then the heart falls into a state of agitation and turmoil. In this state it becomes vulnerable to diseases because it is undernourished and cut off. Cells require oxygen, so we breathe. If we stop breathing, we die. The heart also needs to breathe, and the breath of the heart is none other than the remembrance of God. Without this, the spiritual heart dies.[19]

[19] Hamza Yusuf, *Purification of the Heart: Signs, Symptoms, and Cures of the Spiritual Diseases of the Heart, Translation and Commentary of Imām Mawlūd's Maṭharat al-Qulūb* (Chicago, IL: Starlatch Books, 2004), xvii. This book is a profound commentary on the nature of the

Like the physical organ, the metaphysical heart is strengthened by conditioning or weakened by corrosion. The heart's desire is directed toward God or other than God. When desire is directed away from God, the spiritual heart weakens.

God knows the states of the heart: "Say, 'If you hide what is in your breasts or disclose it, God knows it, and He knows whatever is in the heavens and whatever is on the earth.' And God is Powerful over all things" (Q Āl ʿImrān 3:29). The Qur'an evokes the metaphor of rust corroding the metaphysical heart through immoral action: "But no! That which they [the deniers] used to earn has covered their hearts with rust" (Q al-Muṭaffifīn 83:14). Another verse laments hard-heartedness and describes individuals whose hearts are "like stones, or harder still" (Q al-Baqara 2:74, partial citation). The two kinds of metaphysical hearts are juxtaposed in the following verses in terms of how they receive divine guidance:

> What of one whose breast God has expanded for submission, such that he follows a light from his Lord? Woe to those whose hearts are hardened to the remembrance of God! They are in manifest error.
>
> God has sent down the most beautiful discourse [in the form of] a consistent, reiterative book, whereat quivers the skin of those who fear their Lord. Then their skin and their hearts soften to the remembrance of God. That is God's guidance with which He guides whomever He will; and whomever God leads astray, no guide has he. (Q al-Zumar 39:22–23)

This oft-recited Qur'anic verse beseeches God to bestow guidance on the heart: "Our Lord, make not our hearts swerve after having guided us, and bestow on us a mercy from Your Presence; truly You are the Bestower" (Q Āl ʿImrān 3:8).

Righteousness in action is tied closely to reverence for God. Islamic theological discourse details the correct moral path of one who professes monotheism and many Qur'anic verses, such as the following, outline this path:

> Truly God commands justice, virtue, and giving to kinsfolk, and He forbids indecency, wrong, and rebelliousness. And He admonishes you, that haply you may remember.
>
> Fulfill the pact of God when you have pledged it, and break not your oaths after solemnly affirming them, and having made God a Witness over you. Surely God knows whatever you do. (Q al-Naḥl 16:90–91)

> O you who have faith! Be steadfast for God, bearing witness to justice, and let not hatred for a people lead you to be unjust. Be just; that is nearer to reverence. And reverence God. Surely God is Aware of whatever you do.
>
> (Q al-Māʾida 5:8)

metaphysical heart, desire, and character formation; it interprets a didactic poem of the Mauritanian scholar Muḥammad Mawlūd Ibn Aḥmad Fāl al-Yaʿqūbī (d. AH 1323 / 1905 CE).

These verses – and hundreds more of this nature – emphasize values such as justice, generosity, truthfulness, and perseverance.

In addition to the values and virtues named in these verses, a related overarching moral value that permeates Islam discourse is the concept of gratitude, or *shukr*. Contemplating God's generous provisions for humankind leads a person to experience overwhelming gratitude. In fact, one Qur'anic verse distills the way to elude divine punishment as simply having faith and gratitude: "Why should God punish you if you give thanks and believe? God is Thankful, Knowing" (Q al-Nisāʾ 4:147). Accordingly, theologians speak about gratitude as the wellspring of reverence. Gratitude leads a Muslim to desire to obey God and to earn God's pleasure. Muslim theologians often discuss gratitude (*shukr*) as the antithesis of denial (*kufr*) of God's existence or benevolent nature.

The "straight path" (*al-ṣirāṭ al-mustaqīm*), a metaphor that is ubiquitous in the Qur'an and prophetic teachings, is the joining of correct understanding and correct desire with upright action. The straight path leads the human being to peace, salvation, and success in life and death: "And God calls to the abode of peace, and guides whomever He will to a straight path" (Q Yūnus 10:25). The "straight path" is the way (*dīn*); it is monotheism. The primordial and true human nature (*fiṭra*) is the monotheistic disposition of someone on this straight path that leads to true contentment, realization, and a pervasive peace that derives from living in harmony with the divine command. Another pair of verses commands humankind to repentance, piety, prayer, and worship: "Turn to Him, reverence Him, perform the prayer, and be not among the idolaters, [be not] among those who have divided in their way and become factions, each party rejoicing in that which it has" (Q al-Rūm 30:31–32). Unlike the people who go astray by dividing into factions, the people of repentance, piety, prayer, and upright worship are on the straight path.

The realization of faith and good character is known as *iḥsān*, a word derived from a root signifying beauty (*ḥ-s-n*). The Prophet Muḥammad, in a famous hadith, explains the concept of *iḥsān* in the following manner: "*Iḥsān* is to worship God as if you see Him, for if you do not see Him, He sees you."[20] Another person asked the Prophet Muḥammad to summarize the religion of Islam, to which he replied, "Say, 'I have faith in God,' then become upright."[21]

[20] See *al-Bukhārī* (https://sunnah.com/bukhari:4777) on the authority of Abū Hurayra.

[21] See *Muslim* on the authority of Sufyān b. ʿAbd Allāh al-Thaqafī; this hadith appears in several early collections, including the one compiled by Yaḥyā b. Sharaf al-Nawawī (d. AH 676 / 1277 CE), *Riyāḍ al-ṣāliḥīn* (*The Gardens of the Righteous*), available online at https://sunnah.com/riyadussalihin:85.

The link between pure monotheistic conviction and virtue is paramount in Islamic thought and pious practice.

Given that the primordial human disposition inherently recognizes truth, an individual's state of being is affected by both the signs (*āyāt*) of the linguistically revealed Qur'an and the signs God placed in creation. Some theologians refer to the linguistic signs – that is, the Qur'anic verses – as the inscribed Qur'an (*al-Qur'ān al-tadwīnī*), while the signs in the natural world are the cosmic Qur'an (*al-Qur'ān al-takwīnī*). Ṭhe Qur'an itself evokes the idea of abundant signs in the outer world, beyond the human being, and in the inner world of the human being. The following verse draws a connection between the macrocosm of the universe and the microcosm of the human being: "We [God] will show them Our signs on the horizons and within themselves until it becomes clear to them that it is the truth. Does it not suffice that your Lord is Witness over all things?" (Q al-Fuṣṣilat 41:53).

Approximately 350 verses of the Qur'an reference this concept of God's signs. Accordingly, the Qur'an contains numerous descriptions for reflecting on God's signs (e.g., *tadabbur, tafakkur*, and so forth). The Qur'an also stresses that signs contained in the unfolding of human history are apparent to those who make the required effort to discern them (as in Q *al-Ḥijr* 15:75). Even ways in which human beings manipulate their natural world to derive benefit (e.g., food, clothing, transportation, shelter, and so forth) are regarded as signs of God's benevolence. Though verses detailing God's benevolent nature occur throughout the Qur'an, Sūrat al-Naḥl (Q 16) in particular contains extended accounts of God's provisions to humankind. Examples include the following verses:

> He [God] it is Who sends down water from the sky, from which you have drink, and from which comes forth vegetation wherewith you pasture your cattle.
>
> Therewith He [God] causes the crops to grow for you, and olives, and date palms, and grapevines, and every kind of fruit. Truly in that is a sign for a people who reflect. (Q al-Naḥl 16:10–11)

> He [God] it is who made the sea subservient, that you may eat fresh meat therefrom, and extract from it ornaments that you wear. You see the ships plowing through it, and [this is so] that you may seek His Bounty, and that perhaps you may give thanks. (Q al-Naḥl 16:15)

> And surely in the cattle there is a lesson for you: We [God] give you to drink from that which is in their bellies, between refuse and blood, as pure milk, palatable to those who drink [thereof].
>
> And from the fruits of the date palm and the vine, from which you derive strong drink and a goodly provision. Surely in this is a sign for a people who understand.

> And your Lord revealed unto the bee, "Take up dwellings among the mountains and the trees and among that which they [humans] build.
>
> Then eat of every kind of fruit and follow the ways of your Lord made easy." A drink of diverse hues comes forth from their bellies, wherein there is healing for humankind. Truly in that is a sign for a people who reflect.
>
> (Q al-Naḥl 16:66–69)

> And God has ordained for you a place of rest in your dwellings, and He has made dwellings for you from the skins of cattle, which you bear with ease on the day you travel and the day you pitch camp. And from their wool, and their fur, and their hair, furnishings, and enjoyment for a while.
>
> And God has made shade for you from among that which He created, and He has made places of refuge for you in the mountains. He has made coats for you that protect you from the heat and coats that protect you from your own might. Thus does God complete His blessing onto you, that perhaps you may submit. (Q al-Naḥl 16:80–81)

The provisions detailed in these verses are God's signs for humankind of God's benevolence and compassion. Each verse of the Qur'an itself is also a sign. The people of reflection use one set of signs to explicate the other to arrive at a deeper understanding of the nature of their existence and the attributes of God. In language, in the nonhuman natural world, and within the human being, abundant signs point to God's existence for those who reflect. Contemplating these signs, by God's leave, is an act of worship and leads a person to theological certainty (*yaqīn*). The Qur'an commands: "Worship your Lord until certainty comes to you" (Q al-Ḥijr 15:99).

For some interpreters, the "certainty" mentioned in this verse refers to death itself. Qur'anic verses such as the following speak about the certainty of the moment of death and a person's impending judgment: "God it is who raised the heavens without pillars that you [can] see, then [He] mounted the throne; and He made the sun and the moon subservient, each running for a term appointed. He directs the affair, expounding the signs, so that you may be certain of the meeting with your Lord" (Q al-Raʿd 13:2).

Even the aging of human beings is a sign to contemplate: "And whomever We [God] give a long life, We cause him to regress in creation. Do they not understand?" (Q Yā Sīn 36:68). Another verse emphasizes this life cycle: "God brought you forth from the bellies of your mothers, knowing naught. And He endowed you with hearing, sight, and hearts, that perhaps you may give thanks" (Q al-Naḥl 16:78). Thus, in the Qur'anic worldview, true righteousness, human realization, excellence, and ultimate success in life all flow from proper understanding of the human condition and God as the Singular, True Reality.

By contrast, erroneous understandings of the nature of reality lead a person to various kinds of delusion and corruption. The Qur'an, hadith, and subsequent religious works detail many varieties of moral and intellectual corruption; Section 4 provides a basic overview of core concepts.

4 Compromising *Tawḥīd*: Deficient Understanding of God

The concept of the straight path of monotheism (*tawḥīd*) is well developed in the Qur'an, hadith, and subsequent Muslim scholarly works. So too opposing concepts – such as the denial of monotheism and idolatry in various forms – are also systematized at great length in foundational sources and later works of Muslim scholarship. The Qur'an describes diverse theological beliefs that fall under the rubric of ascribing partners to God (*shirk*), an umbrella term for various forms of idolatry and beliefs that contradict monotheism. Along with detailed discussions of the relationship between right belief, guidance, morality, and divine pleasure, we find extensive discourse on adulterated or otherwise compromised understandings of monotheism in the Qur'an, hadith, and later theological treatises.

The Qur'an describes the follies of human beings and details the many facets of both correct and erroneous understandings of the nature of reality. In this context, light and darkness are oft-repeated themes. Light evokes knowledge, guidance, truth, and prophetic presence. "The Light" (al-Nūr) is a name of God. Darkness is the absence of guidance and truth: "They [those who ascribe partners to God] desire to extinguish the Light of God with their mouths. But God refuses to do aught but complete His Light, though the deniers (*kāfirūn*) be averse" (Q al-Tawba 9:32). God's truth shines through people's false statements and theological deficiencies: "He it is who sent His messenger with guidance and the way of truth to make it manifest over all ways, though the idolaters (*mushrikūn*) be averse" (Q al-Tawba 9:33). The "way of truth" is pure monotheism.

I outline conceptions of God that are notably excluded from the purview of Islamic monotheism because they are causes of "darkness," ignorance, and corruption. I discuss the concept of the association of partners with God, or *shirk*, and other misguided convictions or cases in which human beings deny and attempt to suppress the truth. I begin by outlining how God tests each human being, then I detail the ways in which human beings fall short in this process of testing. I also examine how character flaws – such as heedlessness, self-delusion, and arrogance – lead people to compromise their convictions. Finally, I explain the concept of human accountability and God's displeasure in Qur'anic accounts.

4.1 Tests for Humankind

Each human being, at the deepest state of awareness, recognizes that God is the Greatest being and ultimate Sustainer, according to the Qur'anic discourse. Nevertheless, human beings have the freedom to either act on this awareness or suppress it. God regularly tests individual human beings such that they exercise their will to their benefit or detriment:

> We [God] will indeed test you with something of fear and hunger, and loss of wealth, souls, and fruits; and give glad tidings to the patient –
>
> Those who, when affliction befalls them, say, "Truly we are God's, and unto Him we return."
>
> They are those upon whom come the blessings for their Lord, and compassion, and they are those who are rightly guided.
>
> (Q al-Baqara 2:155–157)

The trials instituted by God determine the extent of a human being's steadfastness: "And We [God] will test you until We know those among you who strive and those who are patient, and We will test your proclamations" (Q Muḥammad 47:31). Tests can come by way of circumstantial difficulties, promptings of the soul, or whisperings of malevolent forces. The testing offers people opportunities to increase the sincerity of their devotion:

> And if God touches you with affliction, none can remove it save Him; and if He desires some good for you, none can hold back His bounty. He causes it to fall on whomever He will among His servants. And He is the Forgiving, the Merciful. (Q Yūnus 10:107)

The Qur'an instructs that this ongoing testing should lead to a profound state of reliance, or *tawakkul*: "And rely on the Mighty, the Merciful" (Q al-Shuʿarāʾ 26:217). Another well-known verse summarizes: "God, there is no god other than Him, and on God let the faithful rely" (Q al-Taghābun 64:13). At the same time, the Qur'an promises that God does not test a person beyond that person's means and offers language for the Qur'anic audience to use to supplicate for lightened burdens:

> God tasks no soul beyond her capacity. She [the soul] shall have what she has earned and be subject to what she has perpetrated. "Our Lord, take us not to task if we forget or err! Our Lord, lay not upon us a burden like You laid upon those before us. Our Lord, impose not upon us that which we have not the strength to bear! And pardon us, forgive us, and have mercy upon us! You are our Master, so help us against the disbelieving people." (Q al-Baqara 2:286)

Life contains many distractions from this straight path and the sincere pursuit of truth. One verse summarizes: "Vying for increase distracts you, until you visit the graves" (Q al-Takāthur 102:1–2). The Qur'an reminds its audience: "The life of this world is naught but play and diversion. Better indeed is the abode of the hereafter for those who are reverent. Do you not understand?" (Q al-Anʿām 6:32). In another instance, the Qur'an asks, "Did you suppose, then, that We [God] created you frivolously, and that you would not be returned to Us?" (Q al-Muʾminūn 23:118). This life is but a phase of the soul's existence and the Qur'an repeatedly emphasizes that human beings should prepare for a moment of individual reckoning: "Surely the Hour is coming; I [God] would keep it hidden such that every soul might be recompensed for her endeavors" (Q Ṭā Hā 20:15).

God's tests for people are adapted to suit each person's particular state of being. The entirety of life is a test; yet at every instance a person makes decisions that either enhance or degrade their spiritual acumen: "As for those in whose hearts is a disease, it adds defilement to their defilement, and they die while they are deniers. See they not that they are tried each year, once or twice? Yet they neither repent nor take heed" (Q al-Tawba 9:125–26).

In a verse that is often commented on in theological treatises, the Qur'an describes how even prophets navigate tests and how people are tried in their interactions with prophets and with revelation:

> And no messenger or prophet did We [God] send before you [Prophet Muḥammad] but that when he had a longing, Satan would cast [some misunderstanding] into his longing, whereupon God effaces what Satan cast. Then God makes firm His signs – and God is Knowing, Wise –
>
> that He might make what Satan casts a trial for those in whose hearts is a disease and those whose hearts are hard – and truly the wrongdoers are in extreme schism –
>
> and so that those who have been given knowledge might know that it is the truth from your Lord, and thus have faith in it, and that their hearts might be humbled before Him. And truly God guides those who have faith to a straight path. (Q al-Ḥajj 22:52–54)

As this verse describes, God tests human beings by allowing the metaphysical promptings of Satan, the accursed one, to influence them.

Islamic thought, however, is non-dualistic regarding divinity and the cosmic forces of good and evil: God has full power over any evil forces.[22] Similarly, rather than following evil promptings, human beings have the option of taking refuge in God and choosing goodness. Many Qur'anic verses describe the moment of recompense and the divine speech to those individuals who served evil rather than God during their lifetime: "Did I [God] not enjoin on you, O

[22] For detailed analysis of theodicy, see Safaruk Chowdhury, *Islamic Theology and the Problem of Evil* (Cairo: American University in Cairo Press, 2021).

children of Adam, that you not worship Satan – truly he is a manifest enemy to you – and that you worship Me? This is the straight path. For indeed he [Satan] has led many among you astray. Did you not understand?" (Q Yā Sīn 36:60–62).

Satan is the main force external to human beings that God permits to exist as an agent of misguidance. However, the Qur'an suggests that multiple other, subsidiary devils are present in the cosmos: "Among humankind are those who dispute concerning God without knowledge and follow every defiant devil" (Q al-Ḥajj 22:3). Though potent, people can readily divert the sabotages of such devils through redirecting conscious attention toward supplication and contemplation of God. The Qur'an instructs:

> And should a temptation from Satan provoke you, seek refuge in God. Truly He [God] is Hearing, Knowing.
>
> Truly those who are reverent, when they are touched by a visitation from Satan, they remember; then behold, they see.
>
> But as for their brethren, they [devils] draw them ever further into error, and then they cease not. (Q al-Aʿrāf 7:200–02)

Unfortunately for human beings, several factors inhibit this ability for God-conscious awareness in the face of evil or ignorance. These obstacles are the subject of Section 4.2.

4.2 Delusion, Denial, and Ascribing Partners to God

Islamic theology is intimately connected to the development of character, and the enterprise of character-building is inextricably linked to the inculcation of correct theological understanding. Proper, fruitful, enlightened understanding leads to upright and diligent praxis; upright praxis leads to correct understanding in a self-perpetuating cycle. Misguided, ill-intentioned, short-sighted understanding leads to lackluster praxis and imprudent praxis leads to faulty understanding, also in a self-perpetuating cycle. Correct understanding and correct action are essential elements of the Islamic way (*dīn*): the two are mutually reinforcing.

Correct comprehension of *tawḥīd* and fully realized conviction are the goals of Islamic learning and character development. By contrast, incomplete understanding, coupled with lax attention to character development, leads to corrupt action. Ideation and action are fundamentally connected in Qur'anic logic, such that someone who does not have correct understanding of the nature of reality is unlikely to have a sound moral compass. One verse explains the extent to which people can go astray: "Truly those who have not faith in the hereafter, We [God] have made their deeds seem fair to them, while they wander confused" (Q al-Nūr 27:4). Another verse expresses a similar sentiment: "And most of them [human beings] follow nothing other than conjecture. Truly conjecture does not avail against the truth in the least. Truly God knows what they do" (Q Yūnus 10:36).

People may have some degree of awareness of their deepest human purpose and aspire to attain God's mercy and favor. Yet these same people may fall short in multiple respects. For these people, the Qur'an provides regular reminders of the need for righteous action alongside faith. For instance, verses such as the following caution against stinginess: "You will never attain piety till you spend from that which you love. And whatever you spend, truly God knows it" (*Āl ʿImrān* 3:92). Alongside tendencies toward ignorance, confusion, and other negative traits, human beings also tend toward argumentation and arrogance. Some people enact a form of willful denial (*kufr*).

The Qur'an frequently speaks sharply of those who engage in the willful denial of truth. One verse even refers to deniers as "the worst of beasts": "Truly the worst of beasts in the sight of God are those who have denied and will not have faith, those among them with whom you made a pact and who then break their pact every time, and who are not reverent" (Q al-Anfāl 8:55–56).

Likewise, many verses of the Qur'an extol those who uphold promises and are truthful in speech. But it is not enough to be truthful in speech. Some individuals speak eloquently about God but are hypocritical in their actions:

> And among humankind is the one whose talk of the life of this world impresses you, and he calls God as a Witness to what is in his heart, though he is the fiercest of adversaries.
>
> And when he turns away, he endeavors on the earth to work corruption therein and to destroy tillage and offspring, but God loves not corruption.
>
> And when it is said to him, "Reverence God," vainglory sinfully seizes him. (Q al-Baqara 2:204–206)

In the Qur'anic account, this tendency toward arrogance is a major stumbling block for humankind. Overcoming arrogance is necessary for those who desire to be humble before their Lord and draw divine pleasure. In its command to prayerful living, the Qur'an describes humility as a key component of a pious disposition: "Remember your Lord inwardly, in humility and awe, with quietness of words, in the morning and the evening, and be not among those who are heedless. Surely those who are with your Lord are not too arrogant to serve Him; they glorify Him and prostrate to Him (Q al-Aʿrāf 7:205–206).

The Qur'an offers a prime example of arrogance in the figure of Satan (Iblīs), who is too haughty to follow God's command.[23] Iblīs, understood by theologians as a *jinn* (a being without material form who has free will), judges humankind to be a lesser creation: "He [Iblīs] said, 'I am better than him. You [God] have created me from fire, while You have created him from clay'" (Q Ṣād 38:76). The arrogance of Iblīs triggers his downfall from God's grace and in his outcast state he vows to bring about the downfall of as many human beings as possible. Human beings are also arrogant among each other and arrogant in their estimations of human capabilities. According to the Qur'an, human beings tend to be argumentative: "And indeed We [God] have employed every kind of parable for humankind in the Qur'an, and the human being is the most contentious of beings" (Q al-Kahf 18:54).

The Qur'an mentions the related tendency of hypocrisy (*nifāq*) dozens of times. One verse condemns the willfully disobedient for their immorality and draws a connection between hypocrisy, stinginess, and lack of faith: "The hypocritical men and the hypocritical women are like to one another, enjoining wrong, forbidding right, clutching their hands shut [in stinginess]. They forgot God, so He forgot them; truly the hypocrites are iniquitous" (Q al-Tawba 9:67). Those who do not venerate God risk being forgotten in this earthly existence and in a future realm, just as they forgot God and God's commands in this human life.

In a dozen verses, the Qur'an evokes the metaphor of a diseased heart to describe those who have shortcomings in their conviction or expression of monotheism. The Qur'an links this idea of a diseased heart to lying, heedlessness, corruption, hypocrisy, and arrogance:

> Among humankind are those who say, "We have faith in God and in the last day," though they do not have faith.
>
> They would [try to] deceive God and the faithful; yet they deceive none but themselves, though they are unaware.
>
> In their hearts is a disease, and God has increased them in disease. Theirs is a painful punishment for having lied.
>
> And when it is said to them, "Do not work corruption on the earth," they say, "We are only working righteousness."
>
> No, it is they who are the workers of corruption, though they are unaware.
>
> When it is said to them, "Have faith as the people have faith," they say, "Shall we have faith as fools have faith?" No, they are the fools, though they know not.

[23] Iblīs is referred to by name in nine surahs: al-Baqara 2:34, al-Aʿrāf 7:11, al-Ḥijr 15:31–32, al-Isrāʾ 17:61, al-Kahf 18:50, Ṭā Hā 20:116, al-Shuʿarāʾ 26:95, Sabaʾ 34:20, and Ṣād 38:74–75.

And when they meet those who have faith they say, "We have faith," but when they are alone with their devils they say [to their devils], "We are with you. We were only mocking."

God mocks them and leaves them to wander confused in their rebellion.

They have purchased error at the price of guidance. Their commerce has not brought them profit, and they are not rightly guided.

(Q al-Baqara 2:8–16) .

Human beings are susceptible to various kinds of corruption, the cumulative effects of which people can readily observe: "Corruption has appeared on land and sea because of that which human hands have wrought, that He [God] may let them taste some of that which they have done, that haply they might return" (Q al-Rūm 30:41). Here, seeing the effects of corruption is a mercy from God and is a reminder to individuals to return to righteousness while an opportunity remains to change course. Yet human beings are also easily distracted and waste energy focusing on inconsequential affairs. The Qur'an laments: "How many a sign there is in the heavens and on the earth by which they pass; yet they turn away from them!" (Q Yūsuf 12:105).

Greed and the hoarding of material wealth are shortcomings to which people are also susceptible: "Say, 'Were you to possess the treasuries of my Lord's mercy, you would surely withhold them out of fear of spending; the human being is ever miserly'" (Q al-Isrā' 17:100). Rather, the Qur'an instructs, "Say, 'In the Bounty of God and His mercy – in that let them rejoice! It is better than that which they amass'" (Q Yūnus 10:59). Avarice distracts the person from his/her divinely ordained purpose. The Qur'an reminds people: "Strain not your eyes toward the enjoyments We [God] have granted certain classes of them, as the splendor of the life of this world, that We may test them concerning it. The provision of your Lord is better and more lasting" (Q Ṭā Hā 20:131). One surah contains a stark reminder about how the love of wealth can corrupt a person's morality and perception: "Woe to every slandering backbiter who amasses wealth and tallies it, supposing that his wealth makes him immortal" (Q al-Humaza 104:1–3). Envy is a related blameworthy trait rooted in dissatisfaction with the divine decree and how God measures out blessings and provision. In the penultimate surah, the Qur'an instructs those with faith to seek refuge in God from – among other types of dangers – "the evil of the envier when he envies" (Q al-Falaq 113:5).

Some individuals do not act out of malice, but they make theological errors that compromise pure monotheism. For instance, many people take *jinn* as objects of worship (as in Q Saba' 34:41). Another common theological error the Qur'an elaborates is the notion that God has offspring. The Qur'an is particularly emphatic about the erroneous nature of this view: "They say, 'The

Compassionate has taken a child.' You have indeed asserted an egregious thing. The heavens are well-nigh rent thereby, and the earth split asunder, and the mountains made to collapse in ruins, that they should claim for the Compassionate a child. It is not fitting for the Compassionate to take a child" (Q Maryam 19:88–92).

According to the Qur'an, trinitarianism is an inherent violation of pure monotheism. Muslims affirm that God has no parts, is not incarnated, and has no progeny. The Qur'an instructs, "Say, 'Praise be to God, who has no child! He has no partner in sovereignty; nor has He any protector from meekness.' And proclaim His Greatness!" (Q al-Isrāʾ 17:111). According to Islamic teachings, human beings do not need a blood sacrifice to be redeemed so there is no need for a sacrificial figure to forgive them for their sins. Sins, and shortcomings generally, are rectified by a process of reconciliation (*tawba*) that allows the individual to recognize the harm and its impacts, seek redemption directly from God, and potentially reconcile with those wronged through some form of restitution and sincere intention not to repeat the wrong.

With no need for a sacrificial figure, Jesus (ʿĪsā) is like the Prophet Muḥammad in that both are messengers of God who convey theological truth and urge people to righteous action. Jesus's status is unique among messengers as he was the only messenger or prophet born of a virgin (the virgin Mary, Ar. Maryam). Moreover, according to the dominant Islamic understanding, Jesus is still very much alive and did not die on the cross but was raised to heaven and will return at the end of time.[24] Each prophet has distinctive qualities and unique circumstances; each is an exemplar calling to monotheism and righteousness.

The prophets are aided and strengthened by God in their missions. Islamic thought maintains that the Holy Spirit (*rūḥ al-qudus*) is not a part of God – God does not have parts; rather, this spirit is an entity created by God and subject to God's command. (Many theologians have understood this Holy Spirit to be the angel Gabriel [Jabrīl], the angel of revelation.) In several verses – those described here and others – the Qur'an describes one of the functions of the Holy Spirit as giving strength to the Prophet Jesus:

> And indeed We [God] gave to Moses (Mūsā) the scripture and caused a succession of messengers to follow him. And We gave Jesus, son of Mary, clear proofs, and strengthened him with the Holy Spirit. Is it not so

[24] For a detailed scholarly account, see Zeki Saritoprak, *Islam's Jesus* (Gainesville: University Press of Florida, 2014).

> that whenever a messenger brought you something your souls did not desire, you waxed arrogant, and some you denied and some you slew?
> (Q al-Baqara 2:87)

A lengthy verse echoes this description of strengthening Jesus with the Holy Spirit and also describes the trials of various prophets, citing the function of the Holy Spirit in supporting the prophetic mission of Jesus specifically:

> Those are the messengers. We [God] have favored some above others. Among them are those to whom God spoke, and some He raised in ranks. And We [God] gave Jesus, son of Mary, clear proofs and strengthened him with the Holy Spirit. Had God so willed, those who came after them would not have fought one another after the clear proofs had come to them. But they differed: among them were those who had faith, and among them were those who denied. And had God so willed, they [the people who subsequently follow the different messengers] would not have fought one another, but God does as He wills. (Q al-Baqara 2:253)

The latter part of this verse describes a core principle of the Qur'anic conception of belief and practice: "There is no coercion in religion. Sound judgment has become clear from error, so whoever disavows false deities and has faith in God has grasped the most unfailing handhold which never breaks. And God is Hearing, Knowing" (Q al-Baqara 2:256). The verse also describes how diversity in religious conviction is part of a divine plan.

According to Qur'anic accounts, people throughout human history have ascribed partners to God by taking created things as gods or by assigning partners to God, in violation of the principles of monotheism. In one verse, the voice of God speaks to human beings directly and laments the deficit in understanding that some people exhibit: "We [God] created you. Would that you affirm it" (Q al-Wāqiʿa 56:57). In several instances, the Qur'an narrates a dialogue between Abraham (Ibrāhīm) and his people who are worshiping created idols instead of God, who created all things. In one instance, the dialogue ensues as follows:

> And recite to them the story of Abraham
> when he said to his father and his people, "What are you worshiping?
> They said, "We worship idols, and we remain ever devoted to them."
> He [Abraham] said, "Do they hear you when you call?
> Or do they benefit or harm you?
> They said, "No, but we found our forefathers doing so."
> He said, "Have you considered what you worship,
> you and your ancestors?
> For they are all enemies to me, save the Lord of the worlds,
> who created me, and guides me,

> and who feeds me and gives me drink,
> and who, when I am ill, heals me,
> and who causes me to die, then gives me life,
> and who I hope will forgive me my errors on the day of judgment.
> (Q al-Shuʿarāʾ 26:69–82).

In these verses, Abraham criticizes his people for blindly following the precedent of their forefathers without benefit. He then proceeds to offer a simple summary of monotheism.

Worshiping objects instead of God, as described in this story of Abraham and his people, is one kind of theological error. However, the concept of *shirk*, or associating partners with God, is much more subtle. For instance, the Qur'an rhetorically highlights how a person's own whims can become an idol of distraction: "Have you considered one who takes his caprice as his god? And God knowingly let him go astray and sealed his hearing and his heart and placed a cover over his sight. Who then will guide him after God? Will you not then remember?" (Q al-Jāthiya 45:23).

Blindness and deafness frequently appear in Qur'anic discourse as metaphors for a willful lack of understanding, for deficits in insight and obedience. The Qur'an asks another rhetorical question and then explains the metaphor: "Have they [human beings] not journeyed on the earth, that they might have hearts by which to understand or ears by which to hear? Truly it is not the eyes that go blind, but it is the hearts within the breasts that go blind" (Q al-Ḥajj 22:46). Another verse highlights the theme of spiritual blindness and the ascription of partners to God:

> Say, "Who is the Lord of the heavens and the earth?" Say, "God." Say, "Then have you taken, apart from Him, protectors who have no power over what benefit or harm may come to their souls?" Say, "Are the blind and the seer equal, or are darkness and light equal?" Or have they ascribed partners to God that they have created in the likeness of His creation, such that their creation appeared with a likeness to them? Say, "God is the Creator of all things, and He is the One, the Paramount." (Q al-Raʿd 13:16)

Among all the kinds of shortcomings human beings manifest, it is perhaps no surprise that relatively few people are on a foundation of guidance, according to the Qur'anic appraisal. To the Prophet Muḥammad, the Qur'an discloses: "And most of humankind, however ardently you desire, are not those who are faithful" (Q Yūsuf 12:103). Another verse with a similar sentiment describes widespread doubt in God's promises: "Truly to God belongs whatever is in the heavens and on the earth. Verily God's promise is true, but most of them [humankind] know not" (Q Yūnus 10:55). Feeblemindedness, arrogance, misguided beliefs, and other negative tendencies are not without consequence; the

Islamic worldview includes an ultimate accounting. This ultimate accounting is the subject of Section 4.3.

4.3 Accountability and Divine Retribution

In Islamic thought, peoples' erroneous beliefs and moral shortcomings lead to consequences; belief and actions will be judged according to God's justice. The Qur'an repeatedly assures its audience of God's flawless accounting: "Truly God does not wrong human beings in the least, but rather, human beings wrong themselves" (Q Yūnus 10:44). According to the Qur'an and prophetic teachings, some deeds and dispositions are recompensed in a person's lifetime; however, individual souls face an ultimate reckoning at the end of time in a moment when morality is weighed and divine justice enacted. This moment is evoked in hundreds of Qur'anic verses: "God, there is no god other than Him. He will surely gather you all to the day of resurrection, about which there is no doubt. And who is truer than God in speech?" (Q al-Nisāʾ 4:87). The return of all created things to God is a recurring Qur'anic theme: "Surely, We [God] will inherit the earth and whatever is on it, and to Us will they be returned" (Q Maryam 19:40). Those who have sincere faith in God are guided by God's light and protected from harm in an eschatological sense: "God is the Protector of those who have faith. He brings them out of the darkness into the light. As for those who deny [God], their protectors are the idols, bringing them out of the light into the darkness. They are the inhabitants of the fire, abiding therein (Q al-Baqara 2:257).

From an Islamic perspective, God's ultimate reckoning determines how well people fulfilled the purpose of their life – that is, did they worship God to ensure their success in an eternal realm beyond the current, manifest realm of human existence? While one's poor character and reprehensible actions in the earthly realm may not be apparent to other people, everything becomes apparent in the realm of the hereafter:

> There and then, every soul shall experience that which she did in the past, and they will be brought back to God, their true Master, and that which they used to fabricate will forsake them.
>
> Say, "Who provides for you from heaven and earth? Who has power over hearing and sight? And who brings forth the living from the dead, and brings forth the dead from the living, and who directs the affair?" They will say, "God." So say, "Will you not then be reverent?"
>
> (Q Yūnus 10:30–31)

God is Judge and Witness. Individuals may not face the full moral consequences of their actions in their earthly existence; rather, God defers justice until the "Hour" of reckoning: "Lost indeed are those who deny the meeting with God until, when the Hour comes on them suddenly, they say, 'Alas for us, that we neglected it!' They will bear their burdens on their backs. Behold! Evil is that which they bear!" (Q al-Anʿām 6:31).

Justice not served in this life is not lost: "To Him is your return all together; God's promise is true. Verily He originates creation, then He brings it back, that He may recompense with justice those who are faithful and perform righteous deeds. As for the deniers, theirs will be a drink of boiling liquid and a painful punishment for having denied" (Q Yūnus 10:4). Goodness leads to enduring pleasure and abundance, wretchedness to enduring misery and deprivation.

The consequences of arrogant denial or wanton distraction extend beyond this worldly life. The Qur'an provides many similitudes to convey the nature and consequences of denying truth, including the following:

> As for those who deny, their deeds are like a mirage on a desert plain which a thirsty person supposes is water, till when he comes on it, he does not find it to be anything, but finds God there. He [God] will then pay him his reckoning in full, and God is swift in reckoning.
>
> Or like the darkness of a fathomless sea, covered by waves with waves above them and clouds about them – darkness, one above the other. When someone stretches out his hand, he can hardly see it. He for whom God has not appointed any light has no light. (Q al-Nūr 24:40–41)

God ultimately ascribes the fate of each person in accordance with that person's chosen beliefs and actions. The Qur'an even suggests that many human beings were created for damnation:

> Whomever God guides, he is rightly guided; and whomever He leads astray, it is they who are the losers.
>
> We [God] have indeed created for Hell many among jinn and human beings: they have hearts with which they understand not; they have eyes with which they see not; and they have ears with which they hear not. Such as these are like cattle. Nay, they are even further astray. It is they who are heedless.
>
> (Q al-Aʿrāf 7:178–79)

The following verses explicitly outline the purpose of human life and the consequences of worldly actions:

> Say, "God do I worship, devoting my religion entirely to Him.

> So, worship whatever you will apart from Him." Say, "Truly the losers are those who lose their souls and their families on the day of resurrection. Yes! That is the manifest loss."
>
> Above them they shall have canopies of fire and below them canopies; with that does God strike fear into His servants. O My servants! Reverence Me!
>
> And as for those who shun false deities and worshiping them, and turn to God, to them [give] glad tidings. So, give glad tidings to My servants,
>
> who listen to the Word, then follow that which is most beautiful in it. It is they whom God has guided; it is they who are the possessors of intellect.
>
> (Q al-Zumar 39:14–18)

In contrast to delinquent human beings who have reasonable cause to fear death, those who contemplate God with sincerity and who complement that contemplation with righteous action have little cause to fear death, unlike those who did not "answer" the call of their Lord: "Those who answer their Lord shall have that which is most beautiful. But those who answer Him not – were they to possess all that is on the earth and the like of it besides, they would seek to ransom themselves thereby. For them there will be an evil reckoning. Their refuge is Hell. What an evil resting place!" (Q al-Raʿd 13:18).

Through contemplating death – and the experiences beyond it – pious individuals increase in faith and longing for a time when it is said, "O you soul at peace! Return to your Lord, content, contenting" (Q al-Fajr 89:27–28). Such verses on human fates give rise to questions of predetermination, free will, and the nature of God's punishment and mercy, all subjects of theological discussion among Muslim scholars. In a concise explanation, God has given each human being contingent will, but to God belongs the command, supreme wisdom, and knowledge of all things. God has given human beings the choice to express faith or to deny monotheism; they may act in accord with morality or stray. Still, human free will (and all human action) is contingent on divine decree: "And you do not will but that God wills. Truly God is Knowing, Wise" (Q al-Muzzammil 73:30). *The Study Quran* offers this concise summary of the Qur'anic perspective on the question of free will versus determinism: "God has willed that human beings have the ability to will, but could remove it at any moment. God wills that human beings will, but does not necessarily determine the content of what they will, meaning that human beings have a limited range of freedom willed by God and that they are ultimately responsible for their own acts."[25]

[25] Nasr et al., *The Study Quran*, 1456, n. 30. For a detailed discussion of free will and related topics in Islamic thought, see Özgür Koca, *Islam, Causality, and Freedom: From the Medieval to the Modern Era* (Cambridge: Cambridge University Press, 2020).

A conviction in ultimate justice and individual moral accountability and the contingent exercise of human will is at the heart of the Islamic worldview. Historian and ethicist Raymond Harvey summarizes: "If human beings, by virtue of their intelligence and free will, are able to despoil the world, so too are they called to act as its stewards."[26] In light of this human exercise of free will, God instructs prophets to deliver a simple message regarding ultimate accountability: "Tell My servants that I am indeed the Forgiving, the Merciful, and that My Punishment is the painful punishment" (Q al-Ḥijr 15:49–50).

Many such verses succinctly sum up the nature of human accountability and the divine recompense: "Faces will be humbled before the Living, the Self-Subsisting. And whoever bears wrongdoing will have failed" (Q Ṭā Hā 20:111). God provides recompense to each soul according to that soul's worldly actions and states:

> The Raiser of degrees, the Possessor of the Throne, He casts the Spirit from His Command on whomever He will among His servants to warn of the day of the meeting,
>
> the day when they come forth with nothing concerning them hidden from God. Whose is the sovereignty this day? It is God's, the One, the Paramount.
>
> One that day every soul shall be recompensed for that which she has earned. No wrong will be done that day. Truly God is swift in reckoning, so warn them of the day of the imminent event, when hearts will be in throats, choking in agony. The wrongdoers shall have no loyal friend, nor any intercessor to be obeyed.
>
> He knows the treachery of eyes and that which breasts conceal.
>
> God decrees with truth, and those on whom they invoke apart from Him do not decree with anything. Truly God is the Hearer, the Seer.
>
> (Q Ghāfir 40:15–20)

Hope remains for human beings who revere God:

> Truly those who are in awe for fear of their Lord,
>
> and those who have faith in the signs of their Lord,
>
> and those who ascribe not partners to their Lord,
>
> and those who give what they give while their hearts quake with fear that they shall return to their Lord –
>
> it is they who hasten toward good deeds and are foremost in them.
>
> We [God] task no soul beyond her [the soul's] capacity, and with Us is a scripture that speaks in truth. And they shall not be wronged. (Q al-Mu'minūn 23:57–62)

God is the Reckoner, but God is kind to those who strive with their faith and actions.

---

[26] Ramon Harvey, *The Qur'an and the Just Society* (Edinburgh: Edinburgh University Press, 2019), 191.

The Qur'an emphasizes God's perfect justice and many verses highlight God's generous accounting: "Who is he who will lend to God a goodly loan? He [God] will multiply it for them, and theirs will be a generous reward" (Q al-Ḥadīd 57:13). Out of generosity, God scales human goodness exponentially: "Truly God commits not so much as a mote's weight of wrong: if there is a good deed, He will multiply it and grant from His presence a great reward" (Q al-Nisāʾ 4:40). By contrast, human beings ignore the signs of God at their peril and false beliefs can lead to even good deeds being worthless in the ultimate reckoning. The Qur'an underscores this dynamic:

> Say: "Shall I inform you who are the greatest losers with respect to their deeds?
> Those whose efforts go astray in the life of this world, while they reckon that they are virtuous in their works."
> They are those who disbelieve in the signs of their Lord, and in the meeting with Him. Thus, their deeds have come to naught, and on the day of resurrection We will assign them no weight.
> That is their recompense – Hell – for having disbelieved and for taking My signs and My messengers in mockery. (Q al-Kahf 18:103–106)[27]

Qur'anic narratives frequently discuss the collective fates of previous peoples who were destroyed and punished because of their arrogance, moral wrongdoings, and mockery of prophets. The pharaoh who ignored the teachings of the prophet Moses is the most frequent Qur'anic example of a tyrant who creates havoc on the earth and who exceeds all bounds with his aspirations for godlike stature. The Qur'an relates the fate of the pharaoh and his companions as a lesson for those who take heed:

> Indeed, the warnings came to the house of Pharaoh.
> They denied Our [God's] signs – all of them; so, We seized them with the seizing of One Mighty, Omnipotent.
> Are your deniers better than those? Or have you some exemption in the ancient scrolls? (Q al-Qamar 54:41–43)

The rhetorical question posed in this last verse invites reflection on the two essential options posed by the monotheistic paradigm of Islam: submit to God willingly or unwillingly.

In summary, within the monotheistic paradigm, God has invested human life (and the broader universe) with purpose and people must strive to realize that purpose amidst distractions and the challenges posed by some of their base tendencies:

> Know that the life of this world is but play, diversion, ornament, mutual boasting among you, and vying for increase in property and children – the likeness of

[27] Other instances of this principle in the Qur'an include Q al-Māʾida 5:5 and al-Furqān 25:23.

> a rain whose vegetation impresses the farmers; then it withers such that you see it turn yellow; then it becomes chaff. And in the hereafter, there will be severe punishment, forgiveness from God, and contentment. And the life of this world is naught but the enjoyment of delusion. (Q al-Ḥadīd 57:22)

The coming of the final judgment, as described in hundreds of Qur'anic verses, separates out those who have enjoyed delusion from those who have followed a straight path and have been granted respite. One such description of the reward of the pious and the regret of the one who strays from monotheism and morality is as follows:

> That day the inhabitants of the garden [paradise] will have the best dwelling place and the most beautiful rest.
>
> And the day when the heavens are split open with clouds and the angels are sent down in a descent,
>
> That day the true sovereignty will belong to the Compassionate [God], and that will be a difficult day for the faithful.
>
> And that day the wrongdoer will bite his hands, saying "Would that I had taken a path with the messenger!
>
> Oh, woe unto me! Would that I had not taken so-and-so for a friend!
>
> He [the friend] did cause me to stray from the reminder after its having come to me, and Satan is a forsaker of humankind."
>
> And the messenger will say, "O my Lord! Truly my people have taken this Qur'an for foolishness."
>
> Such did We [God] make for every prophet an enemy from among the guilty, and your Lord suffices as a Guide and a Helper.
>
> (Q al-Furqān 25:24–31)

Again and again the Qur'an urges people to reflect and have patience: "And We [God] did not create the heavens and the earth and whatever is between them, save in truth. And surely the hour is coming. So, forbear with beautiful forbearance" (Q al-Ḥijr 15:85). Those who are diligent in their devotion and forbear are promised God's pleasure: "Surely those who are faithful and perform righteous deeds, for them the Compassionate will bestow affection" (Q Maryam 19:96). Another verse mentions awe and steadfast virtue as criteria for achieving a divine reward: "As for one who fears standing before his Lord and forbids the soul from caprice, truly the garden is the refuge" (Q al-Nāziʿāt 79:40–41).

As these and hundreds of Qur'anic verses detail, God-consciousness is inextricably linked to moral virtue. Correct theological understanding and upright action are essential in cultivating progressively deeper states of awareness of the nature of God, the human being, and the purpose of the universe. I describe various Islamic practices for developing beautiful forbearance, striving for divine affection, and cultivating knowledge of God in Section 5.

5 Imbibing *Tawḥīd:* Ritual and Contemplative Life

Islamic spiritual praxis is a path toward a fuller realization of *tawḥīd* through contemplation, moral, and intentioned action. From the testimony that "there is no god [i.e., no entity worthy of worship] but God," whispered into a baby's ear or declared by a new Muslim entering the state of Islam, this profession of monotheism is the beginning of a life of commitment as a Muslim. The practitioner then reiterates this commitment to monotheism through multiple spiritual practices, from a forefinger raised in each prayer to the hundreds of iterations of this testimony chanted in acts of devotional remembrance (*dhikr*). The goal of such practices is to cultivate deeper states of experiential knowledge of the reality of divine oneness, as the Qur'an commands: "O you, the faithful! Remember God with frequent remembrance and glorify Him morning and evening" (Q al-Aḥzāb 33:41–42).

Thus far this Element has offered a theoretical exploration of Islamic monotheism. In this section, I examine how the concept of monotheism is embodied in core Muslim practices of ritual worship. Practically speaking, Muslims perform certain actions regularly, or on special occasions, that reinforce the practical, lived implications of monotheism. First, I consider how the awareness of monotheism is cultivated in the pillars of embodied devotional practice. I then consider devotional language about God in the context of individual supererogatory praxis and in life cycle rituals. A great diversity of pious praxis is found among Muslims across history and geography. Section 5.1 highlights core elements of devotional practice that are widely attested to across communities and epochs.

5.1 Pillars of Devotion

The five pillars (*rukn*, pl. *arkān*) of Islamic ritual practice – namely the testimony of faith (*shahāda*), prayer (*ṣalāt*), the wealth tax (*zakāt*), fasting (*ṣawm*), and pilgrimage (*ḥajj*) – train individuals to understand Islamic monotheism. Each pillar of practice purifies the believer's consciousness and desires, continually redirecting an individual toward monotheism (*tawḥīd*). While plenty of resources explain the basic form and function of each pillar, here I attempt to explicate something of their function in helping an individual gain awareness of *tawḥīd*.

The *shahāda* is a testimony to monotheism that begins with the negation "there is nothing worthy of worship (no god)" (*lā ilāha*) and transitions to the affirmative "except God" (*illā-llāh*). The second part of the *shahāda* affirms the prophethood of Muḥammad: "Muḥammad is God's messenger" (*Muḥammadan rasūl Allāh*). Through the affirmation of Muḥammad as the messenger of God (*rasūl Allāh*), the *shahāda* also implicitly affirms the Qur'an as a message (*risāla*) from God to humankind. The *shahāda* is in many respects the simplest of the pillars and the most essential; it is the basis of all subsequent devotional acts. The *shahāda* is the gateway into Islam; its sincere profession is all that is entailed in converting to Islam. The *shahāda* is also the conceptual heartbeat of Islam, with the phrase having a rhythmic quality when articulated: *Ashhadu an lā ilāha illā Allāh wa-ashhadu anna Muḥammadan rasūl Allāh* (I bear witness that there is no god other than God and I bear witness that Muḥammad is God's messenger).

The prayer (*ṣalāt*) focuses the individual's consciousness on piety, morality, and his/her relationship to God.[28] Inextricably connected to the movement of the earth around the sun, it provides the rhythm of daily Muslim life. The prayer functions as a reflective speed bump to prevent heedlessness and to inhibit individuals from recklessly driving through the day. In its words and postures, the prayer conditions Muslims to seek guidance in humility. The Qur'an refers to the person who is vigilant, sincere, and humble in ritual prayer: "What of one who is devoutly obedient during the watches of the night, prostrating and standing [in prayer], wary of the hereafter and hoping for the mercy of his Lord? Say, 'Are those who know and those who do not know equal? Only possessors of intellect reflect'" (Q Ṣād 39:9).

There are a variety of motivations for prayer. Rosina-Fawzia Al-Rawi (Iraqi Islamic studies specialist and spiritual teacher in the Shādhiliyya Sufi tradition) outlines several common motivations, including fear of punishment and hope for reward, reassurance, and recognition of God's Lordship, and love of divine truth and spiritual longing:

> Some pray for fear of punishment and strive for His [God's] reward. Some pray for the sake of praying and say, "When difficulties come, they come out of Your omniscient justice, and when good things come, they come out of Your omniscient grace." And then there are those who pray because the eye of their heart has seen divine truth in its majesty, its beauty, and its perfection, whose hearts have drowned in the ocean of love, their striving dissolved in divine contentment.[29]

Purifying the metaphysical heart causes these inclinations toward worship to become increasingly intense. The prayer is also the ritual pillar that most immediately reinforces the messages of the Qur'an. The recitation of the Qur'an – whether in the context of prayer or at other times, whether individually

[28] For a rigorous overview of the discipline of *ṣalāt*, see Marion Holmes Katz, *Prayer in Islamic Thought and Practice* (New York: Cambridge University Press, 2013).

[29] Rosina-Fawzia al-Rawi, *Divine Names: The 99 Healing Names of the One Love*, trans. Monique Arav (Northampton, MA: Olive Branch Press, 2015), 185.

or in a group – reinforces *tawḥīd* and calls to moral virtue. The Qur'an itself instructs: "And when the Qur'an is recited, harken to it and listen, that haply you may receive mercy. And remember your Lord within your soul, humbly and in awe, being not loud of voice, in the morning and the evening, and be not among those who are heedless" (Q al-Anfāl 8:204–205).

The fast (*ṣawm*), a month-long intensive training in self-control, conditions individuals to endure the arduous pursuit of spiritual refinement. With eyes toward the phases of the moon, Muslims learn to welcome the pangs of hunger and thirst because of their capacity to refocus their consciousness. From the predawn hours until the setting of the sun, for the entire ninth lunar month of Ramadan, those seeking to fulfill the command of God abstain from satisfying the physical appetites for food, drink, and sexual pleasure. In Ramadan evenings, gratitude for bounty radiates, intensified by the periods of restraint. The wider Muslim community, or umma, endures the trial together in a communal act of perseverance and with empathy for those experiencing chronic hunger and food insecurity.[30]

The *zakāt*, a once-a-year wealth tax, helps purify an individual's material possessions. The *zakāt*, for those who possess more than a threshold amount of wealth beyond their needs, is a donation of a prescribed share of one's wealth and property to select categories of recipients. The *zakāt* protects the material security of the vulnerable and supports the functioning of civil society. The word *zakāt* is derived from the verb *zakkā*, which means to purify; those who purify their desires in accordance with the principle of *tawḥīd* receive deliverance and ultimate contentment. The connection between giving of wealth and purification is made explicit in the Qur'an:

> Thus have I [God] warned you of a raging fire,
> which none will enter, save the most wretched,
> who denies and turns away.
> The most reverent will avoid it,[31]
> the one who gives wealth to purify
> not recompensing thereby any for a favor,
> save for seeking the countenance of his Lord, the Highest,
> and surely, he will become content. (Q al-Layl 92:14–21)

The Quran uses the concept of purification (*tazkiya*) not only to refer to the purification of wealth but also to the refinement of the spiritual heart and the soul: "One who purifies her [the soul] has prospered" (Q al-Shams 91:9). In more than two dozen verses, the Qur'an pairs the performance of the prayer

[30] For reflections on the merits of fasting Ramadan in a monotheistic paradigm, see Yusuf, *Purification of the Heart*, 174–86.

[31] An alternate translation is "will be removed from it." A host of other Qur'anic verses describe the reverent as avoiding hellfire entirely.

(*ṣalāt*), with the giving of *zakāt*, thus indicating the central importance of charity and spending of one's wealth in the pursuit of piety.

The pilgrimage (*ḥajj*) hones an individual's consciousness of the reality of human mortality and the possibility for spiritual transcendence in this life, through willing surrender and fleeing toward God for refuge. With its connection to a particular place, namely Mecca and the surrounding area, the *ḥajj* also connects Muslims to the sacred genealogy that has transmitted monotheism through time to the present. It is incumbent only on those who are financially, physically, and circumstantially able to perform it and is to be performed, at a minimum, once per lifetime. The *ḥajj* is demanding and exhilarating, not merely a journey toward and through Mecca, but a journey toward the Real, the True, a journey in which pilgrims profess their desire and enact their conviction with ardent effort. The performance of the *ḥajj* rituals connects the pilgrim to the figure of Abraham, the paradigmatic monotheist who, as the Qur'an narrates at length, goes to great lengths to discern truth and to obey the command of God.[32] Many rituals performed during the pilgrimage function to draw consciousness toward pure monotheism. For instance, a prayer known as the *talbiya*, a devotion inspired by Abraham's spiritual journey, is uttered repeatedly by pilgrims on their approach to the sacred precincts. The statement affirms core aspects of *tawḥīd* and reinforces the pilgrim's singularity of purpose and heightened awareness of God, the Knower, the Guide. According to one possible etymology, the *talbiya* is related to the word *lubb* (essence, core, heart, or intellect). With the recitation of the *talbiya* on route to the sacred precincts in Mecca, the pilgrim directs his/her innermost faculties toward God with utter sincerity of purpose by continually repeating: "[I am] at Your service O God, at Your service. At Your service, you have no partners, at your service. Verily the praise and the bounty are Yours alone, and [to You is] sovereignty. You have no partners." (*Labbayka Allāhumma labbayk, labbayka lā sharīka laka labbayk, inna l-ḥamda wa-l-niʿmata laka wa-mulk, lā sharīka lak.*)

These pillars of ritual practice have their minimum requirements, but they also provide Muslims with opportunities to intensify their devotional praxis: the *shahāda* can potentially be uttered with every breath; there is no specified limit

[32] For a concise and rich account, see Hussein Rashid, "Hajj: The Pilgrimage," in *The Practice of Islam in America*, ed. Edward E. Curtis IV, 60–80 (New York: New York University Press, 2017). For another account of the spiritual merits of the pilgrimage, see Abū Ḥāmid al-Ghazālī, *The Mysteries of the Pilgrimage: Kitāb asrār al-ḥajj*. Book 7 of *The Revival of the Religious Sciences*, trans. M. Abdurrahman Fitzgerald (Louisville, KY: Fons Vitae, 2020). For historical and theological reflections on the significance of the Ka'ba, see Martin Nguyen, *Modern Muslim Theology: Engaging God and the World with Faith and Imagination*, 60–68 (Lanham, MD: Roman & Littlefield, 2019).

on the quantity of *ṣalāt* one may perform; the obligatory *ṣawm* takes place during Ramadan, but fasting on other days is a highly meritorious act; the *zakāt* is a specified share of wealth given once per year, but engaging in generosity, abstaining from attachment to material possessions, eschewing the fear of poverty, and curbing desire for worldly status are all meritorious deeds; the *ḥajj* is a one-time requirement for those who are able, but it may be undertaken more frequently.

Scholarly treatises abound to guide Muslims toward sincerity of devotion, whether through deepening performance the ritual pillars or through additional voluntary works of devotion, such as supererogatory prayers, additional charity, and recitation or contemplation of the Qur'an. Those who teach and inculcate piety often emphasize acts of commission and of abstention to help lead an individual to refined consciousness. The renowned Andalusian mystic and scholar Muḥyī l-Dīn Ibn ʿArabī (AH 560–638 / 1165–1240 CE) describes hunger and silence (acts of abstention) alongside seclusion and vigilance (acts of commission) in a famous treatise, *The Adornment of the Spiritually Transformed* (*Ḥilyat al-abdāl*):

> The pillars (*arkān*) of spiritual knowledge [hunger, seclusion, vigilance, and silence] are complete when knowledge revolves around the acquisition of these four: knowledge of God, of the self, of this world, and of Satan. When man withdraws from the created world and from himself, and when he silences his own internal voice ... and when he relinquishes corporeal nourishment and remains wakeful while others are plunged in sleep: when these four properties have been united in him, then his humanity is transmuted into an angelic nature and his servanthood into mastery; his intellect (*ʿaql*) becomes a sense faculty, his invisible reality (*ghayb*) becomes visible, and his interior becomes manifest.[33]

Supererogatory practices – that is, those beyond the obligatory five pillars – are a way to augment an individual's awareness of the subtleties of God's holiness, of the self, of the world, and of the nature of disobedience (as typified by Satan). Such acts lead to an increase in God-consciousness and enable Muslims to trust in the divine succor, as explained in the Qur'an:

> Only they are faithful whose hearts quake with fear when God is mentioned, and when His signs are recited to them, they increase them in faith, and on their Lord they rely,
>
> who perform the prayer and spend from that which We [God] have provided them.
>
> It is they who are truly the faithful. For them are ranks in the sight of their Lord, and forgiveness and a generous provision (Q al-Anfāl 8:2–4).

[33] [Muḥyī al-Dīn] Ibn ʿArabi, *The Four Pillars of Spiritual Transformation: The Adornment of the Spiritually Transformed (Ḥilyat al-abdāl)*, trans. Stephen Hirtenstein (Oxford: Anqa, 2014), 10.

Striving is necessary on the spiritual path, particularly given that "God alters not what is in a people until they alter what is in themselves" (Q al-Raʿd 13:11, partial citation). The ritual practices help a person develop a refined consciousness and disposition.

5.2 God-Consciousness in Language

In the initial section of this work, I detailed the significance of the names and attributes of God, as outlined in systematic theology. Here, I highlight the centrality of "remembering God" (*dhikr*) as a core aspect of piety. Remembrance of God with the tongue is said to increase remembrance in the spiritual heart and lead to a more intensified knowledge of God and purification of the individual: "He indeed prospers who purifies, [who] remembers the name of his Lord and prays" (Q al-Aʿlā 87:14–15). Nearly three hundred verses of the Qur'an evoke this notion of remembrance with the word *dhikr* (from the root *dh-k-r*), which can mean both to remember and to mention, as in: "Remember Me, and I will remember you; Give thanks to Me and deny Me not" (Q al-Baqara 2:152). Words derived from this root can also mean "to remind," as in: "Remind! You are but a reminder" (Q al-Ghāshiya 88:21). Hence, the practice of *dhikr* fulfills the command to "remember God."

Reciting and contemplating the names and qualities of God are potent entry points through which to foster piety. Islamic pious practice is replete with prayers related to divine oneness or other divine attributes that Muslims can offer as private supplications throughout the day before mundane daily activities such as dressing, eating, sleeping, and so forth. These prayers help prevent mundane activities from becoming profane – many such prayers are reported in hadith as being said or taught directly by the Prophet Muḥammad. Communal gatherings dedicated to practices of remembrance (*dhikr*) have also proliferated worldwide, spurred by patterns of migration and conversion. Various lineages of Muslim spiritual guides recite slightly different prayer litanies that include selections of Qur'anic verses, formulas of praise taught by the Prophet Muḥammad, and recitations of God's most beautiful names. Certain phrases are ubiquitous. Historian Bruce Lawrence describes the significance of the phrase *Allāhu akbar* (God is the Greatest), that is used in the call to prayer, in prayer itself, and in daily devotional speech: "To say *Allahu Akbar* is to invoke Allah above, before, and beyond all others.[34] Other common phrases of remembrance that are part of everyday Muslim speech include the *basmala* (i.e., the words "In the name of God the Merciful and Compassionate"; *bismillāh al-raḥmān al-raḥīm*), *subḥān Allāh* (glory be to God), and *al-ḥamdu li-llāh* (praise be to God).

[34] Lawrence, *Who Is Allah?*, 7.

Life cycle events are also occasions in which Muslims regularly use language evoking monotheism (*tawḥīd*). The celebrations of births, weddings, and funerals are all communal occasions in which God's attributes are proclaimed.[35] Wedding ceremonies, for instance, often incorporate this verse on the nature of God's creation:

> And among His signs is that He created mates for you from among yourselves, that you might find rest in them, and He established affection and mercy between you. Truly in that are signs for a people who reflect.
> (Q al-Rūm 30:21)

Family life, in general, is of the utmost significance in the Qur'anic worldview;[36] upholding familial bonds extends beyond blood relations to the nature of relationships between people. For instance, the Qur'an instructs those who have faith to bind together as siblings, holding fast to "the rope of God":

> And hold fast to the rope of God, all together, and be not divided. Remember the blessing of God on you, when you were enemies and He joined your hearts, such that you became siblings by His blessing. You were on the brink of a pit of fire, and He delivered you from it. Thus does God make clear to you His signs, that haply you may be rightly guided. (Q Āl ʿImrān 3:103)

In the Islamic understanding, God is not just aware of what an individual says in the context of worship. How an individual speaks toward other people is also an essential aspect of piety. Many verses emphasize righteous speech and action as a facet of God-consciousness. For instance, the Qur'an instructs: "And when you are offered a greeting, respond with a greeting that is better, or return it; surely God takes account of all things" (Q al-Nisāʾ 4:86). In other cases, God tests people in their character and resolve through the speech of other human beings toward them: "The servants of the Compassionate are those who walk humbly on the earth, and when the ignorant address them, say, 'Peace'" (Q al-Furqān 25:65). Moreover, those whose spiritual beings are diseased are known by their tone of speech: "And if We [God] willed, We would show them [those who follow that which angers God] by their mark. And you will certainly know them by their tone of speech. And God knows your deeds" (Q Muḥammad 47:30). Even in the context of theological debates, the Qur'an instructs people to maintain decent speech: "Call to the way of your Lord with wisdom and goodly exhortation, and dispute with them in the most virtuous matter. Surely your Lord is He who knows best those who stray from His way, and He knows

[35] For a contemporary ethnographic account, see Juliane Hammer, "Weddings: Love and Mercy in Marriage Ceremonies," in *The Practice of Islam in America*, ed. Edward E. Curtis IV, 165–187 (New York: New York University Press, 2017).

[36] Ibrahim, *Women and Gender*, 66–72.

best the rightly guided" (Q al-Naḥl 16:125).[37] Goodly speech is an essential aspect of Islamic piety. Moreover, explaining *tawḥīd* and enjoining good are regarded as collective obligations upon Muslims.

6 Forty Qur'anic Verses on God's Nature

This section provides a window into the concept of monotheism and the nature of God in the Qur'an by offering a selection of additional verses beyond those cited in previous sections of this Element. Muslim compilers of hadith often use the number forty in their collections, and some mystics consider the number significant. I list the verses by their order of appearance in the Qur'an.

al-Baqara 2:255	God, there is no god other than Him, the Living, the Self-Subsisting. Neither slumber overtakes Him nor sleep. To Him belongs whatever is in the heavens and whatever is on the earth. Who is there who may intercede with Him save by His leave? He knows that which is before them and that which is behind them. And they encompass nothing of His Knowledge, save what He wills. His pedestal embraces the heavens and the earth. Safeguarding them tires Him not, and He is the Exalted, the Magnificent.
Āl ʿImrān 3:26	Say, "O God, Master of Sovereignty, You give sovereignty to whomever You will, and You take sovereignty from whoever You will. You exalt whomever You will and abase whomever You will. In Your hand is the good. Truly You are Powerful over everything."
Āl ʿImrān 3:74	He [God] selects for His Mercy whomsoever He will, and God is the Possessor of Tremendous Bounty.
al-Nisāʾ 4:1	O humankind! Reverence your Lord who created you from a single soul and created from her [the soul] her mate, and from the two has spread abroad a multitude of men and women. Reverence God, through whom you demand your rights of one another, and [reverence] the wombs. Truly God is a Watcher over you.

[37] For a reflection on fundamental principles of interreligious engagement from within an Islamic paradigm, see Celene Ibrahim, "*Sūrat al-ʿAlaq* and Dispositions for Interreligious Engagement," in *Words to Live by: Sacred Sources for Interreligious Engagement*, ed. Or Rose, Homayra Zaid, and Soren Hessler, 82–92 (Maryknoll, NY: Orbis, 2018).

(cont.)

al-An'ām 6:12	Say, "To whom belongs whatever is in the heavens and on the earth?" Say, "To God. He has prescribed Mercy for Himself. He will surely gather you on the day of resurrection, in which there is no doubt. Those who have lost their souls, they have no faith."
al-An'ām 6:59	He [God] is Dominant over His servants. He sends guardians over you, till, when death comes unto one of you Our messengers take him, and they do not neglect their duty.
al-A'rāf 7:56	Work not corruption on the earth after it has been set aright; rather, call on Him [God] in fear and in hope. Surely the Mercy of God is ever nigh for the virtuous.
al-Anfāl 8:24	O you who have faith! Respond to God and the messenger when he calls you to that which gives you life. And know that God comes between a person and his heart, and that to Him you will be gathered.
al-Tawba 9:51	Say, "Naught befalls us, save that which God has decreed for us. He is our Protector, and in God let those who have faith rely."
Yūnus 10:3	Truly your Lord is God, who created the heavens and the earth in six eons, then mounted the throne, directing the affair. There is no intercessor, save by His leave. That is God, your Lord; so worship Him. Will you not remember?
Yūnus 10:5	He it is who made the sun a radiance, and the moon a light, and determined for it stations, that you might know the number of years and the reckoning [of time]. God did not create these save in truth. He expounds the signs for a people who know.
Hūd 11:123	To God belongs the unseen in the heavens and on the earth, and to Him are all matters returned. So worship Him, and rely on Him. And your Lord is not heedless of that which you do.
Ibrāhīm 14:34	And He [God] gives you something of all that you ask of Him, and were you to count the blessings of God, you could not number them. Truly humankind is wrongdoing, ungrateful.

(cont.)

al-Isrā' 17:110	Say, "Call on God, or call on the Compassionate. Whichever you call on, to Him belong the most beautiful names. And be not loud in your prayer, nor too quiet therein, but seek a way between."
al-Kahf 18:58	And your Lord is Forgiving, Possessed of Mercy. Were He [God] to take them [those who do wrong] to task for what they have earned, He would have hastened the punishment for them. Nay, but theirs is a tryst, beyond which they will find no refuge.
al-Kahf 18:109	Say, "If the sea were ink of the words of my Lord, the sea would be exhausted before the words of my Lord were exhausted, even if We [God] brought the like thereof to replenish it."
Maryam 19:65	[God is] the Lord of the heavens and the earth and whatever is between them. So worship Him and be steadfast in His worship. Do you know of any like to Him?
Maryam 19:93	There is none in the heavens and on the earth but that it comes to the Compassionate as a servant.
Ṭā Hā 20:110	He [God] knows that which is before them and that which is behind them, and they encompass Him not in knowledge.
al-Anbiyā' 21:19	To Him [God] belongs whoever is in the heavens and on the earth. Those who are with Him are not too arrogant to worship Him, nor do they [become] weary.
al-Anbiyā' 21:92	Truly this community of yours is one community, and I am your Lord. So worship Me!
al-Ḥajj 22:5	O humankind! If you are in doubt concerning the Resurrection, [remember] We [God] created you from dust, then from a drop, then from a blood clot, then from a lump of flesh, formed and unformed, that We [God] may make clear for you. And We cause what We will to remain in the wombs for a term appointed. Then We bring you forth as an infant, then that you may reach maturity. And some are taken in death, and some are consigned to the most abject life, so that after having known they know nothing. And you see the earth desiccated, but when We

(cont.)

	send down water on it, it stirs and swells and produces every delightful kind.
al-Ḥajj 22:18	Have you not considered that to God prostrates whoever is in the heavens and whoever is on the earth, the sun, the moon, the stars, the mountains, the trees, and the beasts, and many among humankind? But for many the punishment has come due. Whomever God disgraces, none can ennoble. Truly God does whatever He will.
al-Ḥajj 22:38	Truly God defends those who have faith. Truly God loves not any treacherous ingrate.
al-Ḥajj 22:73	O humankind! A parable is set forth, so harken to it! Truly those on whom you call apart from God will never create a fly, even if they joined efforts to do so. And if the fly should snatch something from them, they could not retrieve it from it. Feeble are the seeker and the sought!
al-Muʾminūn 23:78	He [God] it is who brought into being for you hearing, sight, and hearts. Little do you give thanks!
al-Nūr 24:35	God is the Light of the heavens and the earth. The parable of His Light is a niche, wherein in is a lamp. The lamp is in a glass. The glass is, as it were, a shining star kindled from a blessed olive tree, neither of the east nor of the west. Its oil would well-nigh shine forth, even if no fire had touched it. Light upon light. God guides to His Light whomever He will, and God sets forth parables for humankind, and God is the Knower of all things.
al-Nūr 24:41	Have you not considered that God is glorified by whoever is in the heavens and on the earth, and by the birds spreading their wings? Each knows its prayer and its glorification; and God knows that which they do.
al-Furqān 25:61	Blessed is He who placed constellations in the sky and placed therein a lamp and a shining moon.
al-Rūm 30:40	God it is who created you, then nourished you; then He causes you to die; then He gives you life. Is there anyone among those you ascribe as partners who does aught of that? Glory be to Him and exalted is He above the partners they ascribe.

(cont.)

Fāṭir 35:38	Truly God knows the unseen of the heavens and the Earth. Truly He knows what lies within breasts.
al-Shūrā 42:26	He [God] responds to those who have faith and perform righteous deeds and will increase them from His bounty. Yet as for those who deny, theirs will be a severe punishment.
al-Aḥqāf 46:33	Have they not considered that God, who creates the heavens and the earth and did not weary in their creation, is able to give life to the dead? But indeed, He is Powerful over all things!
Muḥammad 47:38	Behold! You are those who are called on to spend in the way of God; yet among you some are miserly. And whoever is miserly is only miserly toward himself. God is the Rich, and you are the poor. And if you turn away, He will cause a people other than you to take your place, and they will not be the likes of you.
al-Ḥadīd 57:21	Race to forgiveness from your Lord and to a garden whose breadth is as the breadth of heaven and earth, prepared for those who have faith in God and His messengers. That is the Bounty of God, which He gives to whomever He will, and God is Possessed of Tremendous Bounty.
al-Ḥadīd 57:28	O you who have faith! Reverence God and have faith in His messenger; He [God] will give you a twofold portion of His Mercy, make a light for you by which you may walk, and forgive you – and God is Forgiving, Merciful.
al-Ḥashr 59:24	He is God, the Creator, the Maker, the Fashioner; to Him belong the most beautiful names. Whatever is in the heavens and the earth glorifies Him, and He is the Mighty, the Wise.
al-Ṣaff 61:8	They [those who fabricate lies against God] desire to extinguish the Light of God with their mouths, but God completes His Light, though those who deny be averse.
al-Taghābun 64:11	No misfortune befalls, save by God's leave. And whoever has faith in God, He guides his heart. And God is Knower of all things.
al-Insān 76:28	We [God] created them [human beings] and made firm their frames; and whenever We will, We will exchange them for others like them.

7 Conclusion

Tawḥīd is a statement on the divine nature, in short, that God is the Originator, the Sustainer, the Knower of everything, the singular Truth and Reality, the One without any partners, any internal divisions, any children, or any need. According to the Islamic understanding, *tawḥīd* is grasped through the innate human disposition (*fiṭra*) and through observation and contemplation of the signs (*āyāt*) that God has placed in the world. *Tawḥīd* is discerned when human beings contemplate these signs – natural phenomena and the wonders of their being itself. In addition to these signs, God has sent revelation (*waḥy*) at various points in human history to foster pure monotheism. The revelations received by prophets – enlightened individuals whom God has commissioned to deliver reminders to their peoples – explicate details of God's nature and urge the faithful to moral action. These reminders often, according to the Qur'an, fall on deaf ears and heedless hearts, save for those who introspect.

Introspection and observation of the cosmos point a person of upright character and understanding toward the creed of pure monotheism. Human beings are created by God with a perfected nature that subsequently may become corrupt due to various forces. Nonetheless, God, as described in the Qur'an, guides and is accepting of sincere repentance. Human beings do not need a blood sacrifice to be redeemed, so there is no need for a sacrificial figure to gain God's forgiveness. There are ultimately no intermediaries between human beings and the Supreme Being. Prophets are moral exemplars and sources of theological guidance.

Inculcating awareness of the divine nature and attributes is the central purpose of Islamic devotion. However, awareness of God is contingent upon the purity of an individual's metaphorical heart, the seat of metaphysical consciousness. Purity of heart, in turn, is achieved by means of divine blessings through the struggle people engage in to overcome egoism and their other negative tendencies. The universe is imbued with a God-given purpose. The extent to which people discern and fulfill their purpose – for human beings, the proactive surrender to God – is the extent to which they achieve life success. True success lies in cultivating piety, and piety entails striving to comprehend the nature of God and to accept wholeheartedly the fundamental state of servitude that constitutes the human condition. Each of the core Islamic ritual practices – the testimony of faith, the practice of prayer, the fasting of Ramadan, the wealth tax, and the pilgrimage – serves to inculcate this awareness and state of being. God-consciousness is further developed through everyday acts of righteousness, such as dignified speech and good relations with people, that allow an individual to develop clarity around matters of theology and morality.

This clarity of consciousness constitutes the beacon of light on the straight path of pure monotheism, or *tawḥīd*. The Cairene spiritual master Ibn ʿAṭāʾ Allāh al-Iskandarī (d. AH 709 / 1310 CE) poetically explains the different levels of God-consciousness and their respective rewards:

> *Tawḥīd* is knowledge, and knowledge is the root of faith, and faith is belief. When the heart believes something, this is called knowledge; and when this knowledge strengthens, it is called certitude; and when it strengthens further still, it is called *tawḥīd*; and when it becomes as firm as a mountain, it is called gnosis [*maʿrifa*].The one who comes to know the inner doctrines of submission to God is like the one who discovers a treasure; the one who comes to know the inner doctrines of faith is like the one who discovers a gold mine; and the one who comes to know the deepest secrets of spiritual excellence is like the one who discovers alchemy.[38]

[38] Ibn ʿAṭāʾ Allāh al-Iskandarī, *The Pure Intention: On Knowledge of the Unique Name (al-Qaṣd al-mujarrad fī maʿrifat al-ism al-mufrad)*, trans. Khalid Williams (Cambridge: Islamic Texts Society, 2018), 9.

Notes on Style and Transliteration

Transliterations from Arabic follow the style of the *International Journal of Middle East Studies* (*IJMES*). Terms that are common in English dictionaries, such as Qur'an, hadith, and surah, are not transliterated. In translating proper names used in the Qur'an, I gloss the Arabic name on the first occurrence and thereafter employ the common Anglicized name. Names for God that are common in Muslim discourse are capitalized. Qur'an citations are abbreviated by the letter Q, the surah title, surah number, and verse number. Verses of the Qur'an are cited in full unless otherwise specified, and citation numbers refer to the widely used 1924 CE Cairo edition. Arabic versions of hadith are sourced from Sunnah.com and cited with reference to that platform's numbering system unless otherwise specified. For dates in premodern Islamic history (i.e., prior to the nineteenth century), I provide the Hijra year (AH, *anno hegirae*) followed by the Common Era (CE) year.

Translations of the Qur'an are primarily from *The Study Quran: A New Translation and Commentary*, edited by Seyyed Hossein Nasr, Caner K. Dagli, Maria Massi Dakake, Joseph E. B. Lumbard, and Mohammed Rustom (HarperCollins, 2015); however, I make slight adjustments in capitalization, punctuation, style, and diction for ease of reading. For instance, I use terms like *humankind* instead of *mankind* and conventional modern second-person pronouns (*you*, *your*) instead of more antiquated ones (*thou*, *thy*). In several instances, I translate a slightly different shade of the lexical meaning of the Arabic word. For instance, I translate *mu'min* and words derived from the root *'-m-n*, as *faith* instead of *belief* to capture the element of trust inherent in the Arabic root. Likewise, where *The Study Quran* translates *kufr* as *disbelief*, I translate the concept as *denial*.

Per convention, masculine pronouns are used to refer to God. This pronoun does not assign a masculine nature or an ontological gender to God; God does not manifest in a male form in Islamic discourses. Moreover, some Qur'anic verses contain statements that pertain to human beings in a general sense and employ the generic pronoun in Arabic (*huwwa*); again per convention, I have retained the generic/masculine pronoun *he* in translation.

Bibliography

Abd-Allah, Umar Faruq. "One God, Many Names." Chicago, IL: Nawawi Foundation, 2004.

Bouguenaya, Yamina. *Living with Genuine Tawhid: Witnessing the Signs of God through Qur'anic Guidance*. Charlottesville, VA: Receiving Nur, 2016.

Chittick, William C. "Worship." In *The Cambridge Companion to Classical Islamic Theology*, edited by Tim Winter, 218–236. Cambridge: Cambridge University Press, 2008.

Chowdhury, Safaruk. *Islamic Theology and the Problem of Evil*. Cairo: American University in Cairo Press, 2021.

al-Ghazālī, Abū Ḥāmid. *The Mysteries of the Pilgrimage: Kitāb asrār al-ḥajj*. Book 7 of *The Revival of the Religious Sciences,* translated by M. Abdurrahman Fitzgerald. Louisville, KY: Fons Vitae, 2020.

El-Tobgui, Carl Sharif. *Ibn Taymiyya on Reason and Revelation: A Study of Dar' taʿāruḍ al-ʿaql wa-l-naql*. Leiden: Brill, 2020.

Gimaret, Daniel. *Les noms divins en Islam: Exégèse lexicographique et théologique*. Paris: Cerf, 1988.

Hammer, Juliane. "Weddings: Love and Mercy in Marriage Ceremonies." In *The Practice of Islam in America*, edited by Edward E. Curtis IV, 165–187. New York: New York University Press, 2017.

Hamza, Feras and Sajjad Rizvi with Farhana Mayer, eds. *An Anthology of Qur'anic Commentaries, Volume I: On the Nature of the Divine*. Institute of Ismaili Studies Qur'anic Studies Series 5. New York: Oxford University Press, 2008.

Harvey, Ramon. *The Qur'an and the Just Society*. Edinburgh: Edinburgh University Press, 2019.

Harvey, Ramon. *Transcendent God, Rational World: A Māturīdī Theology*. Edinburgh: Edinburgh University Press, 2021.

Ibn ʿArabi [Muḥyī al-Dīn]. *The Four Pillars of Spiritual Transformation: The Adornment of the Spiritually Transformed (Ḥilyat al-abdāl)*. Translated by Stephen Hirtenstein. Oxford: Anqa, 2014.

Ibrahim, Celene. "*Sūrat al-ʿAlaq* and Dispositions for Interreligious Engagement." In *Words to Live by: Sacred Sources for Interreligious Engagement*, edited by Or Rose, Homayra Zaid, and Soren Hessler, 82–92. Maryknoll, NY: Orbis, 2018.

Ibrahim, Celene. *Women and Gender in the Qur'an*. New York: Oxford University Press, 2020.

al-Iskandarī, Ibn ʿAṭāʾ Allāh. *The Pure Intention: On Knowledge of the Unique Name (al-Qaṣd al-mujarrad fī maʿrifat al-ism al-mufrad)*. Translated by Khalid Williams. Cambridge: Islamic Texts Society, 2018.

Katz, Marion Holmes. *Prayer in Islamic Thought and Practice*. New York: Cambridge University Press, 2013.

Koca, Özgür. *Islam, Causality, and Freedom: From the Medieval to the Modern Era*. Cambridge: Cambridge University Press, 2020.

Lawrence, Bruce. *Who Is Allah?* Chapel Hill: University of North Carolina Press, 2015.

Lumbard, Joseph. "Covenant and Covenants in the Quran," *Journal of Qur'anic Studies* 17, no. 2 (2015): 1–23.

Morrissey, Fitzroy. *A Short History of Islamic Thought*. New York: Oxford University Press, 2022.

Nasr, Seyyed Hossein, Caner K. Dagli, Maria Massi Dakake, Joseph E. B. Lumbard, and Mohammed Rustom, eds. *The Study Quran: A New Translation and Commentary*. San Francisco: HarperOne, 2015.

Nguyen, Martin. *Modern Muslim Theology: Engaging God and the World with Faith and Imagination*. Lanham, MD: Rowman & Littlefield, 2019.

Rashid, Hussein. "Hajj: The Pilgrimage." In *The Practice of Islam in America*, edited by Edward E. Curtis IV, 60–80. New York: New York University Press, 2017.

al-Rawi, Rosina-Fawzia. *Divine Names: The 99 Healing Names of the One Love*. Translated by Monique Arav. Northampton, MA: Olive Branch Press, 2015.

al-Ṣadūq [Abū l-Ḥasan ʿAlī b. al-Ḥusayn b. Mūsā b. Bābawayh al-Qummī]. *The Book of Divine Unity (Kitāb al-tawḥīd)*. Commentary by Ḥāshim al-Ḥusaynī al-Ṭihrānī, translated by Ali Adam, edited by Michal Mumisa and Mahmood Dhalla. Birmingham, UK: Al-Mahdi Institute, 2013.

Saritoprak, Zeki. *Islam's Jesus*. Gainesville: University Press of Florida, 2014.

Schmidtke, Sabine. *The Oxford Handbook of Islamic Theology*. Oxford: Oxford University Press, 2016.

Trigg, Roger. *Monotheism and Religious Diversity*. Cambridge Elements in Religion and Monotheism. Cambridge: Cambridge University Press, 2020.

Winter, Tim, ed. *The Cambridge Companion to Classical Islamic Theology*. Cambridge: Cambridge University Press, 2008.

Yusuf, Hamza. *The Creed of Imam al-Ṭaḥāwī (al-ʿAqīdah al-Ṭaḥāwiyya)*. Berkeley, CA: Zaytuna Institute, 2007.

Yusuf, Hamza. *Purification of the Heart: Signs, Symptoms, and Cures of the Spiritual Diseases of the Heart, Translation and Commentary of Imām Mawlūd's Maṭharat al-Qulūb*. Chicago, IL: Starlatch Books, 2004.

Acknowledgments

I thank the series editors, Chad Meister and Paul Moser, as well as Beatrice Rehl and her team at Cambridge University Press. My anonymous reviewers provided generous and valuable feedback. Carl Sharif El-Tobgui, my dear mentor, offered detailed insights and suggestions, and Valerie Joy Turner contributed editorial guidance. The Dillon Fund at Groton School provided research support. Nayma Tasnim Islam and Zahra Carol Lee provided encouragement. Ahmed Ibrahim contributed his beautiful patience, and Rahma Ibrahim served as my study companion. *Wa-l-ḥamdu li-llāhi rabb al-ʿālamīn.*

Cambridge Elements ☰

Religion and Monotheism

Paul K. Moser
Loyola University Chicago

Paul K. Moser is Professor of Philosophy at Loyola University Chicago. He is the author of *Understanding Religious Experience*, *The God Relationship*, *The Elusive God* (winner of a national book award from the Jesuit Honor Society), *The Evidence for God*, *The Severity of God*, *Knowledge and Evidence* (all Cambridge University Press), and *Philosophy after Objectivity* (Oxford University Press); the co-author of *Theory of Knowledge* (Oxford University Press); editor of *Jesus and Philosophy* (Cambridge University Press) and *The Oxford Handbook of Epistemology* (Oxford University Press); and co-editor of *The Wisdom of the Christian Faith* (Cambridge University Press). He is the co-editor with Chad Meister of the book series Cambridge Studies in Religion, Philosophy, and Society.

Chad Meister
Bethel University

Chad Meister is Professor of Philosophy and Theology and Department Chair at Bethel College. He is the author of *Introducing Philosophy of Religion* (Routledge), *Christian Thought: A Historical Introduction*, 2nd edition (Routledge), and *Evil: A Guide for the Perplexed*, 2nd edition (Bloomsbury). He has edited or co-edited the following: *The Oxford Handbook of Religious Diversity* (Oxford University Press), *Debating Christian Theism* (Oxford University Press), with Paul Moser, *The Cambridge Companion to the Problem of Evil* (Cambridge University Press), and with Charles Taliaferro, *The History of Evil* (Routledge, six volumes).

About the Series

This Cambridge Element series publishes original concise volumes on monotheism and its significance. Monotheism has occupied inquirers since the time of the biblical patriarchs, and it continues to attract interdisciplinary academic work today. Engaging, current, and concise, the Elements benefit teachers, researchers, and advanced students in religious studies, biblical studies, theology, philosophy of religion, and related fields.

Cambridge Elements

Religion and Monotheism

Elements in the Series

Monotheism and Religious Diversity
Roger Trigg

Divine Ideas
Thomas M. Ward

Hindu Monotheism
Gavin Dennis Flood

Monotheism and the Rise of Science
J. L. Schellenberg

Monotheism and Faith in God
Ian G. Wallis

Monotheism and Human Nature
Andrew M. Bailey

Monotheism and Forgiveness
S. Mark Heim

Monotheism, Biblical Traditions, and Race Relations
Yung Suk Kim

Monotheism and Existentialism
Deborah Casewell

Monotheism, Suffering, and Evil
Michael L. Peterson

Necessary Existence and Monotheism: An Avicennian Account of the Islamic Conception of Divine Unity
Mohammad Saleh Zarepour

Islam and Monotheism
Celene Ibrahim

A full series listing is available at: www.cambridge.org/er&m

Printed in the United States
by Baker & Taylor Publisher Services